WORKING WITH STREET CHILDREN

Working with street children

Selected case-studies from
Africa, Asia and Latin America

YOUTH *PLUS*

UNESCO PUBLISHING
INTERNATIONAL CATHOLIC CHILD BUREAU (ICCB)

The designations employed and the presentation of material throughout
this publication do not imply the expression of any opinion whatsoever
on the part of UNESCO concerning the legal status of any country,
territory, city or area or of its authorities, or concerning the delimitation
of its frontiers or boundaries.

Cover photo: UNICEF/El Siglo/Luis Garcia

Published in 1995 by the United Nations Educational,
Scientific and Cultural Organization,
7 place de Fontenoy, 75352 Paris 07 SP
Composed and printed by Presses Universitaires de France, Vendôme

ISBN 92-3-103096-5

Preface

UNESCO has been actively working, albeit indirectly, for street children for many years, The Organization's efforts in this field have been expanded considerably since the World Conference on Education for All (Jomtien, 1990), in particular via a world programme in favour of street and working children.

However, the stark reality is that governments have traditionally left the plight of street and working children to individuals and non-governmental organizations, including many religious organizations. As a result, there are thousands – no, tens of thousands – of small, uncoordinated but nevertheless highly effective projects throughout the world. The eighteen case-studies presented here illustrate the nature of the work being carried out by these organizations.

Working with Street Children is intended particularly for street children educators, social educators, child rehabilitation project managers, those in charge of the law and the representatives of urban public order. It hopes to reply to the need for dialogue expressed in a questionnaire sent in 1991 to some 180 project managers throughout Africa, Latin America and Asia. It brings together information on education and the way that it is developed within eighteen rehabilitation projects, showing how one can work with and for the children. The project is also addressed to governments and to the general public, to inform and to mobilize human and financial resources.

The projects described here have been identified in collaboration with several partners and specialists from such bodies as the National Commissions for UNESCO, the national offices of the United Nations Children's Fund (UNICEF), the International Catholic Child Bureau (ICCB), CHILDHOPE, ENDA-Tiers Monde and the Salesian Don Bosco Congregation. They have been selected not because they are the best in the world, but because they are indicative of the typical formulae employed in response to the questions most frequently asked by both professionals and the public.

The texts are presented in four parts. Part One looks at seven projects characterized by efforts to ensure the reinsertion of street and working children into their families and/or mainframe society through education. The four projects in Part Two rely on work rather than education in their efforts. The three projects described in Part Three concentrate on improving the situation of the children by teaching them to use the street. Part Four is more concerned with the administration aspects of street children projects. The case-studies are deliberately presented without commentary, allowing the reader to establish his or her own conclusions and parallels based upon personal experience. It is not a continuous narration but a collection of results, designed to stimulate the imagination, raise interest and, if possible, to promote or reinforce the commitment to excluded children.

The ideas and opinions expressed in the case-studies published here are those of the project personnel themselves and do not necessarily reflect the position of UNESCO.

Contents

Acknowledgements

This work could not have been accomplished without the active co-operation of many partners in the field, in particular those responsible for the projects presented.

UNESCO would like first and foremost to thank the International Catholic Child Bureau (ICCB) without whose support the programme Street Children, Working Children and this publication would not have seen the light of day.

UNESCO would also like to thank ENDA-Tiers Monde for its support to study trips to Senegal, the Don Bosco Salesian Congregation in India, CHILDHOPE-Manila in the Philippines, the United Nations Children's Fund (UNICEF) and the National Commissions for UNESCO in the countries concerned.

Finally, thanks are due to Benedict Faccini for his help in editing the manuscript of *Working with Street Children*.

Streets

To the eyes of the very poor, open in dignity,
nothing surprises more
than these thousand and one presences of children
living in the streets
roofless, forced into toil to survive.

Instead of peeping Toms
tut-tutting at banks of screens
filled with the taboo of poverty,
instead of the cheap thrills of words
making a bed of desolation
in daily columns of newspaper print
parading suffering like a show.

Instead, the light footsteps to follow
of those, eagerly patient, endlessly kind,
who attend to the comings and goings of children.
Instead, the words of identity
drawn on the brows of these children to be born
who now may come alive.

The streets that divide our living space
into unsafe passages
do not need indignant cries and tears
but rather the laughter of children,
their myriad comings and goings,
happy with thousands of adults impatient to join
the life of the streets,
teachers whose blackboards
are people
and love.

JEAN-PIERRE JUNG, ICCB
1 March 1994

Introduction

Street and working children are a common sight these days in cities around the world, especially in the poorer regions of the South. Deprived of the joys of a normal childhood and adolescence, many of them die early in a state of extreme poverty, or from bullets full of hatred. Those who escape struggle to survive, roam the streets or waste away in despair, relieving their suffering by escaping into the imaginary in an often self-destructive way. Wanting to live, despite the odds, they lead a gloomily ignorant and dangerous existence on the streets. They can be counted in their millions, living with neither roof nor rights, without ever having been to school or having dropped out early. When adult, they will be illiterate or, at best, uneducated. In the meantime, every day is a cycle of torment: hunger, thirst, risky and poorly paid jobs, disease, loneliness, lack of affection, police harassment, legal red tape, institutions, sordid prisons, drugs, slavery disguised as housework or even bare-faced slavery, prostitution, sexual abuse and terminal diseases such as AIDS that come as a result. Merely to understand or combat this apparently incontrollable, growing and unbearable phenomenon, one must ask oneself: What are the root causes? Who are these children? Where do they come from?

Who are they?

The expression 'street children' is not universally accepted. Some, for cultural reasons, find it gives the street the image of being dangerous and immoral. The street, especially in hot countries, is a special place in which the child can socialize. Others find the expression limited, because it attempts to apply to all marginalized children. Others still find it demagogic as the reality portrayed is not as extreme as it seems.

In the same way, the expression 'working children' hides two sides of the same issue. Firstly, most street children only survive thanks to small but lengthy and tiring jobs. They can therefore be described as working children, but they are, in some way, 'free'. Secondly, there are the children excluded from a normal childhood by the work they do to help their family. They are made to work by their parents or do so with their consent. These children are also working children yet there exists no agreed and satisfactory definition of the two aspects. Individuals and associations concerned by this phenomenon perceive it in the particular way that interests them and wrap it in specific terms. So the expression, 'street child' is a kind of blanket term that applies to a multitude of problems. For theoretical or practical purposes – situation analysis or humanitarian intervention – a clear terminology is coming to light. Children may be 'from', 'in', 'of' or 'on' the street. This helps define the relationships that exist between the child and its family, society, the law, public order and the type of help required. From an educational point of view, these groups are the 'missing children', those of an age to be at school but who find themselves outside any social, educational, or even reinsertion, institution. They escape part or all of the social control normally applied to children of their age. They are, by and large, boys (girls being often reclusive and therefore invisible) of between 5 and 18 – varying according to the age of adulthood in each country. They have differing ties with their family – some stay in touch, others are completely cut off, others again are in direct conflict. Their surroundings are the city, its streets, its wastelands, its stations, ports, car parks, hotels, supermarkets or the narrow alleyways that make their way through the poor areas and slums. The concept of the street is polymorphous, it is an area of survival, a 'non-place'. The children live there all or part of the time, night or day.

Where do these children come from and why?

These children come from urban families, sometimes in the city for generations. The families are generally poor or experiencing marital problems. They come increasingly from rural communities and minority ethnic groups in the neighbouring countries, from settled nomads living on the outskirts of cities – the slums. They arrive to escape long droughts or other natural problems. They also belong to political or religious minorities who have been excluded from the development of their countries, or even rejected from formal schools in their home countries for mostly economic reasons. They have, more or less, lost their sense of individual identity and the habitual reference points of social life. If they are to be given a unanimous definition, it would be that they are children in a precarious situation, battling to survive in an urban or semi-urban environment and who behave in an often delinquent way in their efforts to find help.

The fact that poverty is the main cause of this situation is universally accepted. It cannot, however, be the only cause. What about various economic policies, the way social institutions function or even the fact that children from wealthy families find themselves on the street?

How many of them are there?

Here there is no accepted figure either. Estimates vary according to the programmes or the intervention projects. Those who speak of street children in the strict sense of the word, that is to say, children without family or any institutional protection, limit the number to a few hundred, even a few dozen in each city. If those children in difficult situations, who survive on the meagre income of the street or have a vague familial or institutional relationship, are added to this first group, then the total number would exceed 100 million.

Action on the street

Is the phenomenon so incontrollable? It would appear so. Most state institutions seem powerless, overwhelmed or hesitant. Happily, there is also some positive action. In the last forty years, certain people have spoken out against this urban tragedy, and the indignant are struggling to mobilize material and human resources to combat the enormity of the issue.

Nevertheless, these efforts depend on goodwill and charity funds which are, necessarily, insignificant in comparison to the extent of the problem. The numerous policies of intervention currently in practice are only alternative solutions to a social problem that extends much further. In order to hope to solve this

Over 100 million children all over the world are struggling for survival.
These street children are carrying a heavy load of
firewood on their way to the market. Photo: *UNICEF/Shehzad Noorani*

problem one day, these alternative solutions need to be replaced by alternative solutions which take the whole social reality into consideration. If 'education for all' is to be attained, then alternative solutions have to come to an end.

In this respect, it is encouraging to note that, since 1991, more and more states are not only signing the Convention on the Rights of the Child but are also establishing new codes for child protection and defence. More significant on a world level is the ten-point resolution adopted on 4 March 1994 by the General Assembly of the United Nations (at its forty-eighth session) inviting all states and international governmental and non-governmental organizations to increase their efforts to find definitive solutions to the problems and suffering facing street children.

As street children and working children are virtually excluded from governmental educational budgets, it is organizations and individuals who, for the last few decades, have been seeing to the immediate and urgent needs: health, hygiene, safety, family reinsertion if possible, daily food, temporary shelter or guidance centres, clothes, legal advice, protection against violence, unjustified repression and abuse, small jobs, resolution of legal issues, drug advice and, in certain cases, apprenticeship and admission or re-admission to school.

There are many of these non-governmental organizations, both religious and secular, which, alongside the United Nations organizations such as the International Labour Organization (ILO), the World Health Organization (WHO) and the United Nations Children's Fund (UNICEF) or regional elements such as the European Community, try to offer these children the chance to escape their condition.

UNESCO action

Since the 1960s, UNESCO, thanks to its links within the United Nations system, has indirectly contributed to these private efforts for many years. Since the 1990 World Conference on Education for All (Jomtien) and the World Declaration on Education For All, it has done so in a more direct way. According to the declaration, 'Basic education should be provided to all children, . . . Underserved groups – the poor; street and working children . . . should not suffer any discrimination in access to learning opportunities.' (Art. 3). This declaration confirms the importance of education as the best way to pull children out of the cycle of poverty and ignorance and, also, to combat the phenomenon itself at its socio-economic roots.

To this effect, UNESCO, alongside UNICEF and the non-governmental organizations – the International Catholic Child Bureau (ICCB) is one of the most involved – has set up a world programme in favour of street and working children. This programme for fundamental education and professional training comprises three areas of activity: public information, mobilization of financial resources and co-operation on fieldwork. Established after two years of investigation and numerous consultations with professionals, the programme aims, in the most direct and concrete way, to see to the children's educational needs and to the needs of the fieldworkers: street educators, legal and public order representatives (police staff and judges), special psychiatrists for children in difficulty and social workers in general. Among the varying services offered to children by civilian society, education appears to be the most difficult to implement, manage and finance within the rehabilitation structure. How does one convincingly integrate a helpless and socially excluded child into the education process? How can the child be kept within a formal or informal educative cycle? What forms of education should be suggested? How, at the end of the process, can one help the child to join society? How can one prevent the child from slipping into despair again? How can one be sure that the educational approach favoured by the educator is suitable? How can one stop children within high-risk communities from joining the street? These are some of the technical questions that perturb the educators. It is upon this basis that UNESCO organizes its fieldwork programmes.

Part One

Reinsertion through education

There is no single method, no single miraculous solution, to the problem of street and working children. There are, on the other hand, numerous personal and collective efforts aimed at rehabilitating children. Education might appear to be one of the most traditional means of reintegrating a child into society, but the diversity of method and subject-matter shows how innovative and successful education can be with street and working children.

The Loreto Day School in Sealdah, India, has managed to fight the problem of overcrowded classrooms and poor resources in an original way – by educating children as teachers, whom it then sends out to remote areas and slum quarters to teach the illiterate. So far some 600 child teachers have brought literacy to 10,000 children. The school was the winner of the 1994 UNESCO-backed Noma literacy prize. Another approach is taken by the Concordia Project in the Philippines which actively prepares deprived children for entry into formal state schools. It offers alternative teaching which shows the children 'how to be' rather than what to be or what to learn. Learning becomes a participatory activity and lessons draw directly on the street children's experience of urban poverty and survival. Another Philippine project, the Community of Learners, brings parents and children together in an educational experience in which history, social interaction, acting and literacy are all equally important. The centre proves that teaching, especially when dealing with street children, must go beyond the textbook and the blackboard to reveal a whole new world of possibilities and interests.

Formal and conservative schools with their organization, rules and order are not really designed to meet the psychological and educational needs of street and working chilren. Each project described in this part either formulates its own education programme or hopes to mould the children so that they can fit back into the state system of education. Education not only teaches the child to assume a past life spent on the street, it also – at whatever level – empowers the child and opens up a world of hope.

The act of learning is as important as the knowledge absorbed. This theory is clearly taken up in the Bouaké project in Côte d'Ivoire where the notion of success or failure does not exist. In Peru, at the CEDRO Project, the organizers observe that a child fresh off the street is not going to have a particularly long attention span. That is why teachers are not necessarily seen as educators but rather as facilitators, understanding the child's background. A child can learn the meaning of trust and friendship just as well as he or she can learn scholastic skills. What is important is to reveal a different vision of the world, in the words of the DAARA of Malika in Senegal: 'make these children active promoters of development'.

Succour for youth

The Hostel of Hope, Cameroon

Who are they, these 'Nanga boko', 'fighters', 'old campaigners', 'mosquitoes' and 'young 'uns'?[1]

- They are the deprived children and young people of Yaoundé, the capital of Cameroon, escaping difficult or intolerable family situations.
- They are children and young people from northern Cameroon, Chad and the Central African Republic, fleeing from a life of poverty.
- They are youngsters attracted by the false lure of the city, who end up fighting for survival as best they can.
- They are adolescents who go around in gangs, who have carved out their 'operation zones'.
- They are youths who have come in the hope of making a good amount of money before going back home in a blaze of glory.

---

1. The 'fighters' are minors detained in prison; the 'old campaigners' are minors who are former detainees, often multiple re-offenders; the 'mosquito' label refers both to children under 14 detained in police stations for minor offences (they are very mobile and have been caught in the act of 'biting', i.e. snatching, goods) and to street children in general; the 'young 'uns' are children under 10 (their average is from 6 to 8) who are lost or have been abandoned.

What do they do? How do they live?

- They spend their nights in makeshift shelters, eat when they can, smoke any cigarettes they can get, take various forms of drugs, drink alcohol.
- They are often ill and many suffer from chronic bronchitis.
- Hunger follows them everywhere.
- There has been a complete breakdown in communication with their elders, and they seem unable to join in any common venture.
- They have lost all confidence in themselves.
- Failure at school or inability to continue with their studies for financial or other reasons have given rise to a feeling of frustration.
- Delinquency, in some way, alleviates this sense of failure and gives them a certain standing in the eyes of their peers.
- They are many, but they are marginalized, economically, socially and culturally.

The light of hope

February 1977: 'A flame is born and is beginning to spread to wherever it can bring some warmth to the heart of an abandoned child.'

In 1977, the light of hope was lit for many deprived young people in Yaoundé and in the central prison of Kondengui. This includes those who have been released without anywhere to go and those temporarily detained in city police stations. Many are small children lost or rejected by their parents, surviving in police stations. Others are children who have committed some petty theft and are sheltered by someone before returning to their parents. And then there are all the street children who, in one way or another, are beyond the control of the family, that is, when they have one.

It was in February 1977 that the Hostel of Hope, a non-profit social charity, was founded under the auspices of the Diaconal Service of the Archbishopric of Yaoundé. Its objective was 'to organize and co-ordinate the reception, protection, social reinsertion and follow-up of minors in moral danger'. Activities are carried out in collaboration with the various services concerned, both public and private.

The management of and overall responsibility for the Hostel of Hope have been entrusted to an Administrative Committee. Those with administrative and educational responsibilities are named by the Archbishop of Yaoundé and voluntary members are co-opted as needed.

Grants made by the Bishops' Conference and other gifts received are managed by the chief administrator with his committee within the framework of the various projects and smaller undertakings (such as minor constructions and improvements to premises, educational and other materials, subsidies, etc.).

Families who agree to take into their homes, on a temporary basis, one, two or even three young people in difficulty and to treat them as if they were their own children form the basis of the family cell reception structure. They are called 'guardians'. In this way the Hostel of Hope does its best to prepare the children for reinsertion into the family circle by providing them with an infrastructure consisting of small, educational action units, family-type cells, both artisanal and rural, which are as close as possible to the rhythm and the family lifestyle into which the child will eventually be integrated. It is, however, out of the question to allow this transition stage to cover a long period, since this would make reinsertion or 'reimplantation' into the child's own family more difficult.

In the case of a newly freed prisoner, the length of the stay depends upon the availability of the supervisors. For those who are ill, the length of the required medical treatment is considered. The length of a stay depends, too, on the time needed for the social services to contact the families of a lost child or to help a young person settle certain administrative matters (obtain a national identity card, or arrange for transport, etc.). When the child comes from a seriously defective family background and the well-being of the child requires it, the transition period can be extended.

The members of the team know that the reimplantation process is difficult and that it can end in failure. They are, none the less, convinced it is in this way that the child can be helped to grow up, make his or her mark and finally become independent. Thus running away from home is not regarded as an offence but rather as a sign of instability and of lack of confidence. The reasons for this fear need to be found and treated; however, a hostel is an open house – nobody is obliged to stay.

Similarly, if the child finds it difficult to adapt to life in the guardian's home, the chaplain has to take the necessary measures, either by accompanying the child to another guardian or else by returning the child to his or her own family. Whatever solution adopted, it is presented as a positive move, arrived at with the agreement of the child, never as a rejection.

Within this reception structure, the young people retain a certain freedom as to the location of the welcoming home as well as to financial arrangements and mutual responsibilities.

*Over 100 million children all over the world have been left to
the streets, and they are in terrible danger of violence, sexual exploitation,
forced labour, drugs, hunger, solitude, contempt and disease.
Most have never been to school.*

Photo: © *Alain Pinoges/CIRIC*

A 'homely' welcome

According to Monsignor J. B. Ama, Suffragan Bishop of Yaoundé, legally responsible for the Hostel when it was founded, 'It is not a question of performing an act of charity with the children, where they expect to receive everything without active participation on their part.' Far from being weighed down by rigid institutional structures, the Hostel encourages a family atmosphere in which each individual feels responsible for his or her own development. Since its ultimate goal is that of self-development, external aid, whether financial or in kind, should be seen as no more than a topping up grant and not as a budget subsidy intended to cover all expenses. The Hostel and its members in this way avoid becoming permanently dependent upon assistance.

The children's time is occupied in the mornings by training in the workshops and in the afternoons by school classes. The Hostel's primary goal, though, remains the reinsertion of the children into their families and, desirable though they may be, training and schooling of the children is not the aim. If this were the case, there would be a danger that the number of children welcomed would be limited and that some parents might see in this a pretext for avoiding their responsibilities. The Hostel is developing a number of support activities, including preventive measures and follow-up schemes. It also organizes co-ordination meetings, awareness-raising and study sessions on the problems facing these youngsters.

Parents are expected to provide bedding, soap and other toiletries for the child as well as some pocket money. Small though it is, this participation is seen as an indication of the family's interest in the child, but it is never a condition of admission.

A variety of options

The desire to find a personalized, family-type response to the needs of young people in difficulty and the aim of helping them find fulfilment explains the diversity of places and infrastructures available to them. This is all the more important since it is the children themselves who make the choice in accordance with their needs. According to their circumstances, young people can take advantage of one or other of the options made available by the Hostel of Hope.

One branch of the Hostel of Hope, the Mvolyé Hostel, receives children who wish to return to a normal family lifestyle and to go back to their own families.

The Hostel of Hope has built or renovated a number of lodgings for families ('guardians') who have agreed to take in children who have drifted into delinquency. A contract is established with each guardian under which the renting of the lodgings is linked to an agreement to take responsibility for two or three minors. One house, however, is reserved for the temporary accommodation of minors for a period of observation before they are entrusted to a guardian or reinserted in their own families.

Only children who have just come out of prison or been released from police detention are entrusted to receiving families. However, prisoners can take advantage of this arrangement if, when applying for provisional liberty whilst awaiting trial, they give an undertaking to remain with the receiving family.

A young person is accepted into a family after a request, made spontaneously by the young person concerned, has been presented by the chaplain/co-ordinator to a guardian and the latter has accepted it. This spontaneity is important – the Hostel of Hope wants to avoid any notion of imposed 'placing'. If the child is lucky enough to have a family guarantor in the city or in the neighbourhood, he or she is obliged to spend the weekends with that guarantor in preparation for eventual full reinsertion into a family circle.

All the young people prepare for reinsertion by taking part in a variety of activities (manual work in the workshops, in the fields, in the kitchen, keeping the premises clean and tidy, sport, etc.) whilst benefiting from benevolent supervision aimed at identifying their problems and desires for the future.

The Hostel's chicken farm contributes to the goal of self-financing the running of the Hostel whilst at the same time providing a suitable preparation for reinsertion into rural life for children ill-adjusted to the urban environment. Sharing the work of producing subsistence and cash crops (banana growing, etc.) offers an opportunity for a child to become accustomed to working under supervision, to take part in a healthy activity and to prepare for active life. It also helps generate income for the Hostel.

Children who want to acquire the rudiments of carpentry are sent to a carpenter in Yaoundé; since his workshop is equipped with high-quality tools and machinery, they must be able to read and write before they can be apprenticed to him.

Once a week, the Hostel throws its doors open to all and its activities are accessible to everybody. On average some thirty children take advantage of these open days. The staff of the Hostel handle various health matters and administrative formalities, organize educational or horticultural activities and accompany the young people to their receiving families as well as to potential employers. They also handle all the necessary contacts with the administrative, public and private services.

In 1992, a total of 245 children stayed at the Mvolyé Hostel for the first time, for periods of varying length. Some of them were able to be accompanied to their own homes or sent back by train or other means of transport. Others, unfortunately, returned to the streets.

A service known as 'Noah's Ark' was created to meet the needs of minors in prison or those recently released, as well as street children.

The first step was to provide a medical consultation service, available one day a week, for an average of twenty-five minors held in prison. This offered them an opportunity to relax, to be listened to and, in some cases, to renew contact with their families.

After this, the Hostel of Hope participates, within the central Kondengui prison itself, and in particular in the educational centre for young people. Here some fifty young detainees can take advantage of educational and leisure activities (preparation for school examinations; shoe-making workshop; manufacture of bags, etc.; various forms of sport; and television). These activities are led by adult prisoners and the materials used are supplied by the Hostel of Hope and the Chaplaincy service. Each week, the minors receive some food aid from the Hostel of Hope. Since 1977, almost 2,500 minors in the Yaoundé central prison have benefited in this way. Three times a week, a Hostel nun visits the Mfou prison, providing a link between some twenty minors and their families.

Apart from these activities within prisons, Noah's Ark each week receives a dozen or so young people who have just been released or are on the streets. For a few weeks, the Hostel offers them the opportunity to do odd jobs (such as making breeze-blocks or planting vegetables), thus giving them the time to plan their immediate future (return to their families, re-entry into school, serve an apprenticeship with an artisan, etc.). After that, Hostel members follow them up on the street, within the framework of the Prevention Club, or visit and support families temporarily lodging one or two young people in their homes.

The village of Nkoa-Mbang

The inhabitants of this village have become aware of the need to take in young people in moral and physical difficulty. Several volunteer guardians live there and receive young people in their homes, in particular those termed 'mosquitoes' and 'young 'uns', that is to say the youngest at the Hostel. The families receive a certain amount of assistance in this work, usually in the form of food.

Action on the street

Since August 1992, the Hostel of Hope has had a foothold on the street – small premises, let without charge, in the city centre. Seminarists and volunteer members of the Hostel take it in turns to man this post two hours a day, six evenings a week. The street children and young people who live in the area have got into the habit of going there. They know that they will always receive a warm welcome and, if need be, have treatment for any minor ailments, be able to watch television or even just exchange a few friendly words.

When a vehicle is available for their use, some of those manning the premises go to other areas of the city frequented by street children (the main market, the Mfoundi market and the central railway station) and have a chat with the children they already know, meet newcomers, dispense medical treatment for minor ailments, and attend to wounds received in street fights and to a variety of infections. Sometimes cases have to be taken to the Hostel or hospital for treatment. In addition, a nurse is on hand to treat those in need of health care at a clinic every Wednesday afternoon near the central railway station.

The Elig Essono Centre

The multipurpose centre at the Elig Essono chapel, fitted out with the help of the street children themselves, offers leisure and cultural activities (including a film club). It is open to all young people, without distinction, so as to encourage a general mixing of all categories of young people and thereby avoiding the image of a centre for delinquents. Its aim is as much prevention as a form of follow-up care for children who have had a spell in the Hostel. In fact, the cafeteria is run by a former Hostel boy.

Running and maintenance costs are, in principle, covered by the sale of membership cards and entry tickets for the film club. On Wednesday evenings, children requiring medical attention are tended there.

Members of the Hostel of Hope also attempt to establish contact with children employed to watch over parked cars and as general helpers at the central market. Although they are a very unstable, elusive group, every effort is made to reach them through the Elig Essono cultural and leisure clubs. They sometimes come accompanied by their parents.

Since 1977, some 1,250 children and young people have been welcomed at one or other of the facilities established by the Hostel of Hope. Given the constant comings and goings between the Hostel, the street and the family, Hostel members estimate that about 10,000 children have passed through their hands.

A certain approach to education

The total education of the child remains the central concern of the project. The educational director and his team co-ordinate all the Hostel's activities, and the project's approach is under constant review.

The concept of education which guides the Hostel can be summed up in the statement 'The educator is a guide who helps people find their place in society: a person who educates you does this, not by his words, but with his whole being. The children convert us by provoking us.'

Real confidence and a permanent dialogue have to be established between the educator and the young. The young people must learn to be proud of their work and personal efforts. The educator teaches the children about the demands of life and of society and, at the same time, he discovers how to help them. Respect for other people's property is one of the moral precepts inculcated into children and young people. For example, the educator watches to ensure that they do not wear clothing that does not belong to them or receive money without letting their guardian know. Experience shows that young members of the 'underworld' try to tempt them by 'helping them out' with stolen goods.

Although most of the young people express a strong desire to receive training, they find it extrememly difficult to follow and persevere with training of a scholarly nature. Any opportunity for training is then a direct remedy for and response to delinquency. Training of this nature, in the form of evening classes or educational discussions, is not scholarly or 'imposed' but human and responsible with a view to the greater maturity and enhancement of a person's self-esteem. Experience shows that this training must be more practical than theoretical. Educators lay great stress on the help the most advanced pupils can give to the most backward, believing that the best educator one child can have is another child.

School activities enable young people to make certain discoveries, such as the joy of reading, which accompany the effort of learning to write. Children are proud to realize their potential and to have new openings and projects.

The chief educator also fulfils the function of chaplain to prison minors. He is particularly involved in individual and group pedagogical discussions, educational activities (the library and literacy), leisure activities (open-air sport), artistic activities (theatre, cinema, music and song), manual activities (drawing and do-it-yourself tasks) and spiritual teaching (Bible groups). At the same time, he ensures that urgent needs are met (food aid and health) and that the necessary approaches are made to the children's families and to the various official bodies with a view to preparing the child's reinsertion into family and society.

The development of a family atmosphere is essential in the Hostel of Hope, the key element helping these children out of their predicament. The young people, often accustomed to sleeping anywhere, become aware that they now have a 'home'. It is through taking part in a family life, in a healthy climate, that they are able to make the necessary effort to rid themselves of bad habits such as idleness or drug abuse. Leisure time is also important, the cultural and sporting activities encouraging young people to mix and interact.

None of these activities is expected to produce immediate, positive results. They are part of an overall progression towards the child's fulfilment. Everything must be done to enhance the child's self-respect and sense of his or her own worth. When a

All children who work sell part of their childhood,
but never as much as when they are led into prostitution
or practise it to survive.
Photo: *German Commission for UNESCO/Irmela Neu-Altenheimer*

child's reinsertion into his or her family is brought about under favourable conditions, a small party may be organized and the child presented with a 'good conduct certificate'. This enhances children's standing in their own eyes, in the eyes of their families and even, if necessary, in the eyes of the law.

The Hostel of Hope is a diocesan, and therefore a denominational, undertaking. In a multi-denominational context, its aim is to respect each individual's conscience, without any religious discrimination. It is seen as important not to divorce spiritual education from the overall education of the individual.

The Hostel of Hope encourages all forms of concerted action leading to fundamental research into the child in physical and moral danger. At the Hostel's instigation, the Friends of the Hostel (the services of the Ministry of Social Affairs, of the Prison Administration, of Justice, of Health, of Youth and Sport, and the Police, as well as various sociocultural organizations and information agencies) meet periodically to discuss the problems of juvenile delinquency, and the moral and physical difficulties facing street children, and to ensure collaboration between the various services.

Future prospects

Until recently Cameroon experienced a period of economic expansion. Today, however, as in many other countries, its days of prosperity are over. The increasingly unsettled social situation and growing unemployment are creating difficulties for many families. All this is pushing young people towards delinquency and leading to an increase in the number of children living on the streets. In 1992 alone, over 1,000 young people, living on the streets or in the shadow of the prison and the police station, were followed up by the Hostel of Hope and over 100 were received into families.

Over the last few years, the project has stressed the prevention aspect and activities in the open are now taking on increasing importance. The Hostel of Hope would like to multiply its smaller operations so as to make more people aware of the problems of street living and bring organizers together to enable them to exchange experiences and co-ordinate their actions. At the same time, the Hostel wants to retain its decentralized, family-based, reception system. Its leaders feel that it would be illusory to think that only impressive undertakings with imposing buildings and large financial resources will be able to resolve these young people's problems and encourage their reinsertion into society. They argue that experience tends to demonstrate that it would be better to increase the number of smaller operations with the maximum participation of the young people themselves, pointing out that these mini-operations can be rapidly set up to meet precise, topical needs and that their effect is immediate.

Children who come to the city in the hope of making money but who are interested neither in the Hostel nor in reinsertion into their families still need to be cared for on the streets.

Among the small operations being envisaged for the future are a small car wash, with a café/restaurant attached, which would be run by the children and overseen by supervisors in liaison with the Hostel; increasing the number of educators available at strategic points of the city; creating some kind of savings bank to which the children could entrust their earnings; and setting up other centres similar in style to those already operating.

The lost ones

Équipe d'Action Socio-Éducative
en Milieu Ouvert (EASEMO),
Bouaké, Côte d'Ivoire

Some 400 kilometres north-west of Abidjan lies Bouaké. With 2.5 million inhabitants, of whom 45 per cent are under the age of 25, it is the Côte d'Ivoire's second largest city. It is also an important rail centre and the focal point of trade with Burkina Faso.

What has happened to the Côte d'Ivoire's famed 'economic miracle' of the 1950s and 1960s? The economic growth was accompanied by an equally strong population rise and rapid urbanization, then an ever-increasing flow of immigrants eager to have their share of the cake. Unfortunately, growth without development can have surprising effects. First, there is a breakdown in the traditional structures and increasing inequalities between regions, followed by a transfer of profits and revenues out of the country and an increase in public debt. Finally, the price of cocoa collapses (with coffee, cocoa is the country's main resource) and harvests are bad. And there you have yet another country in crisis.

So what has all this got to do with Bouaké and street children?

'My name is Sirambo. My father was from Burkina Faso and I grew up there. My mother was of the Baule people. When I

was 11, I went to live with my grandfather. I didn't like it there, so I left.[1]

'I went to my old man's village. My aunt's husband didn't like me. He made me work all day long in the fields. When I got home there was nothing left to eat. He beat me. I began to steal. Things were going wrong. One day, I set out for the Côte d'Ivoire.

'I was taken in by the head of a bank. He gave me everything I wanted. I was much better off than with my family. Then, he wanted to get to know my family. I took him to my aunt's house. He wanted me to stay with her. So I left for Daloa.

'I found work. I earned a lot of money. Then I started to steal. I went to prison. I was tried and I admitted I was guilty.'

Sirambo's story is similar in many ways to those of many Bouaké street children.

'My name is Simse and I am from Burkina Faso. My mother has married another man and my father has also re-married. I did not get on with my stepmother, so, one day in 1991, I left home, jumped on a goods train and came here.'

'My name is Doko and I am 13 years old. I come from Bougouanou. I came to the railway station thanks to my friend Séa. We offer to help people with their luggage. This is how I get money to eat. When there is no work to be done we walk around.'

'I am 13 years old. My name is Abou. My family is from Bouaké but I don't sleep at home. My mother is dead and my father has a new wife. My aunt sent me to the Koranic school, but I left. My big brother caught me and beat me with a piece of wire.'

'My name is Chaka and I am 14 years old. I work at the bus

---

1. Passages in italics indicate observations made by people participating in the project, members, staff or children.

station and transport depot. I have lost my parents. My big brother used to look after me. He works in transport, in Guinea.'

'My name is Koame and I am 17 years old. I went to school up to Grade 5 at Ouele, in the Daloa Department. I have money problems and my family are poor. My father works for a company in Abidjan.'

The first split comes with adolescence. There is incompatibility with the traditional education system, the lure of the urban mirage, the desire to find work and to earn a lot of money.

'I wanted to set up in trade between Burkina Faso and here, but that requires a lot of money. So I am saving up. A man I know looks after my savings for me.

'I have an uncle in Bouaké. I used to live with him, but I was not happy there. Now I am here, at the railway station, trying to earn a little by carrying people's luggage. I would like to set up in trade, but it's not going too well now. I can't steal, and I'm not interested in drugs. If I knew of anyone who would employ me I would work to save up a decent sum of money.'

They regret leaving school because they realize that study is necessary.

'At home I was always having trouble with my aunt. They used to beat me, and when I went to school, because I'd had to wash the dishes and sweep out the living-room, I was always late and the teachers would not let me in. When my father came, my aunt told him about all this and he beat me. After that I ran away.

'If I had to give a pupil advice, I would tell him: "My friend, the most important thing is to study. If you study and you get on well in class, you will not have the problems I have. OK; but if don't study you will be expelled. At least try to stick with your parents. But unless your old man has got himself another wife who is really kind, you may well have the same problems as I have." '

The children and adolescents want a home and someone to trust and support them.

'I came to the railway station and then I met my friend Séa. He showed me this place. He told me "Children work and sleep here." It is good for earning money, but it is not a good place to sleep because it is not calm enough.

'It would be good if I could find someone to get me started trading between Burkina Faso and the Côte d'Ivoire. Business interests me. A man I know, a Baule, like me, looks after my money for me.

'At first, I carried luggage, but then a man took me on to guard the cars that he sells. I sleep next to the cars. I watch over them and then I also carry luggage.

'My mother's side of the family could help me, but my mother herself has nothing. I shall have to leave and take my chance.

'I would like to go back home, but with my uncle . . . '

They often feel misunderstood, excluded and the object of suspicion.

'One day a woman lied about me. She said I had stolen from her. I was taken away and kept in gaol for three days. When I came out I became ill. I had headaches. I am going to look for some kind of work. When I was small I wanted to become a shoeshine boy.'

Though the details of these stories differ, certain constants recur. All these street children have learned to live from day to day, if not from moment to moment. They all have dreams for the future but are unable to make them come true. They have lost confidence in adults and refuse their authority. They suffer from their isolation, from rejection by their families and society, and feel the need to find or create gangs in which they will be recognized and given a sense of security. At the same time, they run away every time a problem arises. Because they have a negative vision of society and a low image of themselves, they find it difficult to accept any constraints other than those imposed by their peer groups. As Daouda, a former street child says: 'The street never rejects children, it is always proud of them and remains their best friend.' Their rallying points are those where that they can scrounge a few pence or scraps of food – markets, shopping centres, railway stations, coach stations, cinemas and so on.

Negative though these aspects may be, they are offset by the great potential these street children represent. They have enormous inner resources which enable them to face up to exclusion, humiliation, suffering and imprisonment. In the fight for survival they have developped a will to adapt and a sense of solidarity. Moreover, they show great creativity in avoiding difficult situations and in coping with their own, organized little world with its specific organization, hierarchy and customs.

In the Côte d'Ivoire, as in other African countries, a lot of children drop out of school for both social and economic reasons. Many families do not have the resources to bear the high costs of schooling (uniforms; items such as books, pens and paper; and school fees). Furthermore, the absence of sufficient school places and teachers means the demand cannot be met. The selection process has to be strict. Without teacher and parental support, some pupils are then excluded because of low results or because they are unable to keep up with the class. Others are expected to follow traditional practices and interrupt their studies to help their parents in the fields or to take up an inheritance.

Many street children have never been to school or have come from the Koranic schools (50 per cent of those in the EASEMO project; their ages range from 8 to 23, with a majority within the 8-to-15 age bracket).

In almost every case they have been victims of problems that are widespread in changing African societies where tradition and modernity rub shoulders in a state of disequilibrium (polygamy, large families, families without structure, or disunited and separated, men and women on their own, child-mothers, widows and widowers, divorced couples or others living in a state of permanent conflict). The control once held by tradition has been weakened by the surrender of the extended family's power.

In Bouaké, 50 per cent of the street children in contact with the EASEMO project come from completely impoverished families, 40 per cent from families of modest means and 10 per cent from the comparatively well-off class.

Flexible aid

Various public and private attempts have been made to assist street children, in particular by the Maison de l'Enfance, a charitable institution run by the Diocese of Bouaké for children from 8 to 14. Some of the children, however, cannot adapt to its rigid regime and prefer to return to the streets. Furthermore, it has only thirty places to offer and this capacity is no way near sufficient.

Faced with this situation, a woman member of the Association Française des Volontaires du Progrès and a Côte d'Ivoire social worker employed at the Maison de l'Enfance had the idea of creating another centre with flexible structures and better adapted to the young's needs. Enfants et Jeunes de la Rue was born.

Initially placed under the Ministry of Social Affairs, the project was officially established in December 1984 and its management entrusted to the Direction Régionale des Affaires

There is no way street children – abandoned, exploited,
ill-treated – can call for help. The only voice they have is our voice.
Their only hope is our ability to react.
Without an address, street children have no access to school.
Photo: *Hien Lam-Duc*

Sociales de Bouaké. In October 1986 it was renamed EASEMO, Équipe d'Action Socio-Éducative en Milieu Ouvert and was installed in the Social Centre at Bouaké. In the same year, an agreement was signed between the Ministry of Social Affairs and the French Association of Volunteers for Progress. The latter were requested to allocate a person, experienced in working with street children, to train the local personnel. In February 1989, premises built by the Ministry of Social Affairs were allotted to the project. Since May 1990, the French Association of Volunteers for Progress has acted as an intermediary between the project and outside funding agencies. The project is now under the tutelage of the Ministry of Health and Social Protection. The staff has increased (two social workers, three education specialists, two teachers and literacy instuctors).

The EASEMO team begins each day with a meeting. The members exchange news and discuss the previous day (particular cases are examined and possible re-orientation of, or adjustment to, various activities and/or specific actions). On Monday mornings, the team concentrates on the plans for the week; Thursdays are devoted to team meetings and Friday afternoons to an assessment of the past week. Overall assessment of educational activities is achieved by means of monthly, half-yearly and yearly evaluations. The vital criterion is improvement in the street children's behaviour, that is to say, their progress towards reintegration into society.

Although EASEMO is under the authority of an official branch of the administration, the team has the advantage of having a special horizontal hierarchical structure. This means that management of the team is entrusted, in turn, to each of its members on a weekly basis. The team have been given the right, by prefectural decision, to work flexible hours.

The project used to rely on financial and material support from the Ministry of Social Affairs, the French Association of Volunteers for Progress, Maison de l'Enfance and the Swiss branch of Terre des Hommes. The Ministry's financial contribution, however, gradually decreased until, in 1989, it stopped completely. The project continues to function thanks to external aid from the Swiss branch of Terre des Hommes and the personal contributions of the staff (equipment maintenance, fuel and office supplies).

EASEMO as intermediary

The Ministry had fixed a number of priority objectives for the twelve-year period from 1974 to 1986 – mediation between the young people and their families; preparing for their prison release; obtaining administrative documents (birth certificates, national identity cards, consular cards). The general objectives of the project are broader since they cover the social reinsertion of the children, the prevention of and the struggle against all forms of marginalization, and the fight for street children's rights to development (health care, education, training, leisure activities, food, a place to live, etc.).

The training and social reinsertion prescribed by the supervising Ministry are, by no means, incompatible with the project's own specific approach, which may seem original. EASEMO bases its programmes on 'individual life projects'. These are, therefore, variable, and they depend upon the needs of the young people and the possibilities the team has to offer. There is no idea of a predetermined programme. In fact, the team concentrates more on the training aspect (particularly as funding for training is available from the Swiss branch of Terre des Hommes).

The team often calls upon the assistance of external partners such as the Baptist mission and the St Camilla Association. It also seeks to expand the solidarity network and widen its knowledge of the formal sector by, for instance, organizing socio-educational events.

The project team, basically, seeks to act as intermediary between the children and other institutions, organizations and groupings, and through evolving educational strategies to help the young draw up and put into effect individual life projects which will enable them to take total, long-term responsibility for their own lives.

A question of confidence

Even though they may be wary and distrustful, some young people in difficult situations prove to be receptive to adults trying to help them. This openness means that are three basic ways in which children can be sought out: (a) within their own milieu (the team goes out to meet the young, on the streets or in prisons (between 1987 and 1991, release from prison was obtained for forty-one young people)); (b) through chance encounters; and (c) in the course of night patrol visits. In this way, from 1984 to 1992 a total of 320 young people in difficulty, aged 8 to 23, were sought out. Of these, 224, or 70 per cent, have been enrolled.

Sometimes young people are recommended to the team by colleagues, partner agencies or parents – 20 per cent of the young people are recruited in this way. Some young people (10 per cent of total recruitment) come to the Centre of their own accord.

Once the first step has been taken, the Centre must be in a position to respond to the relational, educational and health needs of each young person. To do this, the first task is to get to know the child better. So a private discussion takes place either at the child's home or at the Centre or in the course of activities such as games, hygiene sessions, clothes-washing or other manual activities. A member of the team listens as the young person tells his story and evokes his needs or hopes for the future. The salient points of this interview form the basis for any educational project by the young person and the educator.

The various games (draughts, *pétanque, awalé,* ludo, etc.) all freely available to the children at the Centre have the advantage of reassuring the young people, giving them confidence, allowing them to shrug off tensions and get to know each other. Games also help them develop other qualities – a sense of conviviality, self-control, the ability to dominate emotion or feelings of anguish and the desire to surpass themselves.

Other cultural, sporting and recreational activities (such as games of football in the woods at Kongondékro or the organization of annual fêtes at the Social Centre) enable the young people, like all other children of their age, to experience some moments of joy and relaxation.

At any one time, there are about 150 children and young people, in extremely difficult situations, involved in educational and artisanal training activities.

No miraculous recipe

There is no miraculous recipe for helping young people to escape the street's tentacular grip. But, at least, the project team tries to act rapidly and provide solutions to the most obvious problems or immediate needs – to protect the street children from police harassment, and provide them with affective security and a roof over their heads. After the initial conversation and the enrolment of a child, the educators approach the parents to facilitate any chance of a return to the family. Those who have no family in the area are lodged either in a room or with substitute parents.

Food and clothing are paid for with a small grant of money (400 CFA francs a day). The young people have to manage this money themselves with the help of team members responsible for their follow-up.

After meeting these immediate and vital needs, the team can then prepare for the next stage by trying to see to the children's educational needs. Several options are open to them:

- Young illiterates found in the street are entrusted to the Maison de l'Enfance which manages their literacy training.
- Those children whose intellectual capacities and age make it possible are helped to enter or re-enter the formal school system.
- Initiation courses in functional literacy and arithmetic are given at the Centre. They are intended to enable young illiterate apprentices to acquire the simple, useful basics in reading, writing and arithmetic. The course has the advantage of providing a sense of shared experience between the young and adults, and this is no small help to a young person in difficulty. In addition, bearing in mind the negative effects of earlier failures encountered by many young people, it gives them the opportunity to live through a worthwhile experience. The materials needed for this activity (books, exercise books and pencils) are funded by donations from local partner agencies. The classes last one hour and are held every other day after apprenticeship training.

- Some young people take part in the training of others or in making decisions about them.
- During the school year, schoolchildren who play truant or run away are taken back to their families and counselled again (i.e. brought back up to the appropriate level and followed up).

Each young person is a special case. Finding solutions to problems and planning individual life projects (conception, elaboration, execution and evaluation) involves collaboration between the child and the educators. The children's participation is the Centre's leitmotif, a constant preoccupation.

With decisions concerning the youngest children, the team usually asks for the help of the 'seniors', those who know them and have already lived through the same experiences. This makes it possible to pinpoint the difficulties facing street children and to respond to them. Simon, a young shoemaker who has recently set up in business, now trains other young people and provides a good example of this type of participation and the multiplier effect it can have.

It is always important to establish an exchange situation (between young people and their teachers, and between the young themselves). Each young person thereby lives out realities other than his own. This approach aims to develop adaptability, awareness and self-responsibility.

The project team has two approaches in handling talents, motivations and interests:

1. An interior approach which involves the participation of at least one team member. Here it is a matter of preparing the young person for apprenticeship by setting a number of professional standards to be respected, such as punctuality, assiduity, initiative or respect for personal hygiene (the

Centre has a utility room which the young people use to wash both themselves and their clothing).

2. An exterior approach aims to encourage young people to meet and mix together, and relies on recreational outings, games and market-gardening. The young people use the space around the Centre to grow a variety of crops including lettuce, tomatoes, carrots, groundnuts, gombo, maize and igname, acquiring a taste for manual and agricultural work. Tools such as hoes, rakes, hose-pipes and sprays are provided by the Centre. All this makes it possible for 80 per cent of the activities to take place outside the Centre.

The team also runs group sessions and offers lecture/debates on themes thought to be of major concern to most young people (such as sexually transmissible diseases). The meetings are held at the Centre or in a place chosen by the children themselves. The pedagogical equipment needed for this type of activity is often borrowed or donated by ENDA Jeunesse-Action or the Swiss branch of Terre des Hommes. For some subjects the team calls upon the solidarity network. On health matters, for instance, the team may first demonstrate how to give first aid and then request more general information from the health solidarity network.

A real marathon

The individual follow-up carried out during the early period of attendance at the Centre enables the street children to face up to the rejections, hang-ups and difficulties they previously experienced without feeling that they are on their own. However, the primary objective of this follow-up is to prepare them for apprenticeships in the hope that the desire to learn a trade will emerge. Many street children are quick to ask to be trained even if they have not fully grasped the constraints that apprenticeship poses. Placing them in apprenticeships is the conclusion of a long haul which may take several months or even a full year. For the team, the most difficult problem during this period is to ensure that the young people remain 'in play', and that they have the feeling that they are making the choice of their own free will.

For the project team, arranging an apprenticeship or getting a child back into school means finding a suitable training place or school, carrying out actual placement or reinsertion, resolving any disputes that might arise within the workplace, and following-up and evaluating professional or scholastic progress. If everything is to work well, it is essential for every stage to be prepared in great detail.

It is considered vital that the young person seeking an apprenticeship fully understands the need to accept a certain number of essential rules of conduct (politeness, body and clothing hygiene, etc.). Only if these conditions have been accepted can he or she set out on the apprenticeship-seeking marathon:

The search. Would-be apprentices set out in search of a workshop. After meeting the artisan, they report back to the team on the results of their inquiries.

The negotiations. These lead to the signing of the apprenticeship contract giving access to training. Two possibilities may arise: either (a) the artisan agrees to accept the young person as an apprentice. The team, the artisan and the parents (if there are any) discuss how the contract is to be put into effect; or (b) the artisan requires that the request be formulated in the presence of an adult so as to clarify his responsibilities towards the young person in the workshop. The team and/or the family, the artisan and the potential apprentice agree on a verbal or written contract.

Becoming an apprentice. Once the contract has been signed, a first basic set of tools has to be bought at a cost of about 15,000 CFA francs. Each new apprentice receives a grant for basic necessities of 12,000 CFA francs per month. The apprenticeship expenses (the payment made to the trainers) also have to be paid. All this funding is supplied by the Swiss branch of Terre des Hommes.

Follow-up. Members of the team visit the young people at their apprenticeships. They follow their evolution within the working context (adaptability, punctuality and application), assess the professional knowledge they are acquiring, and give both the apprentice and the trainer moral, psychological and material support (resolving disputes, paying apprenticeship costs, etc.). This follow-up is important since although the thirty-eight artisan trainers participating in the scheme are not professional teachers, their participation in the scheme means that they have to assume the educator's role. This is why the team continues to give professional training to the young as they obtain qualifications to set up on their own or to find employment in local businesses. With this in mind, the team is looking for funding to train and set up young people. It is also constantly seeking deeper knowledge and understanding of the formal sector (business undertakings) with a view to giving children entry into production units.

The final evaluation. At the end of the period the artisan/trainer draws up a balance sheet of the professional knowledge the apprentice has learnt and assesses his/her capacity to exercise the trade whilst observing the rules (respect for customers, workers and trade, punctuality, honesty, etc.). Some artisan/trainers give their apprentices a certificate of professional proficiency.

Once all these stages have been passed, the former apprentices are found jobs or look for work to make them materially independent. If they want to set up on their own, a further series of stages has to be completed:

Pre-installation. This is a transitory period between being an apprentice and becoming a fully fledged artisan. During this period the former apprentice, now qualified, continues to work for the artisan teacher/boss whilst accumulating the equipment needed for the future workshop.

Final installation. At last the former apprentice is installed in the workshop. During a first phase, the functioning and management of the workshop are organized with the help of the EASEMO team. It organizes working hours, the allocation of tasks, staff, documents on income or expenses, the preparation of bills and receipts, and the opening of a savings account. During a second phase, the team retains only the right of inspection.

'Many are called, but few are chosen'

Despite its eight years' experience and the diversity of its activities, the EASEMO team has reached only a minority of its target population (there are some 700 young people in difficult situations in Bouaké). There are a variety of reasons for this:

- A lack of sufficient games and similar activities to make the project a pole of attraction for young people.
- The impossibility of giving all the young people who come to the Centre the benefits of the basic 'first aid' they need often

leads to a feeling of discouragement and a decision not to come to the Centre any more.

- The impossibility of satisfying all the demands for professional training or even of helping all those who have completed an apprenticeship to set themselves up.
- A lack of means to inform and alert the general public and, above all, young people who find themselves in precarious situations.
- The material inability to respond to requests for help from young people who have come out of prison and want to return to their families, most of whom are not resident in Bouaké.
- A lack of resources (fuel and operating funds).
- A lack of co-operation from the parents of young people in difficulty.

To this should be added the fact that the workload involved leaves little time for the reflection needed to elaborate more effective methodological and educational tools. In this respect, it is to be hoped that further information and research into young people in difficulty will propose new ways of thinking and innovative, better adapted, practical measures that could be applied in the field.

Finally, the EASEMO team's answer to questions about success or failure is simply that it rejects these words, preferring to think in terms of successive stages reached in the process of reinsertion into society.

Yes, it takes time to become better acquainted with these 'young sparks'. It takes time for them to change. It takes time, too, to hear what they have to say.

'Now it's finished. I am a shoeshine boy. I go to church and I sleep at the pastor's house. I listen to what others have to say and I tell them my story so that they won't do what I did. I have no money, but now I have joie de vivre.*'*

Brotherhood

The Undugu Society of Kenya

The origins of the Undugu Society of Kenya (*'undugu'* means 'brotherhood' in Swahili) go back to 1972, when the founder, Father Arnold Grol, a Dutch Catholic missionary, was sent to Nairobi.

Father Grol soon became aware of the large number of so-called 'parking boys' roaming the streets. These were the street children, some addicted to sniffing petrol or glue and smoking *bhang,* all surviving on a variety of small odd jobs. There are also 'parking girls' on the streets of Nairobi, but they are less visible than the boys. Most of them work as house-girls or prostitutes, as scavengers on rubbish dumps or in restaurant kitchens.

Determined to do something to rehabilitate these children and guide them towards a change of lifestyle, Father Grol first attempted to capture the interest of parking boys within his parish through sport and recreational activities.

These activities were promoted at a series of Undugu Youth Centres, which formed the organization's initial infrastructure. After two years, the need for a more closely co-ordinated system to pursue the parking boys rehabilitation was recognized and it was realized that rehabilitation could be achieved in ways that went far beyond sport and other forms of recreation. The Youth Centres were, therefore, consolidated into a single organization

– the Undugu Society of Kenya, whose prime aim was 'the rehabilitation of parking boys into useful members of society'.

Since its establishment, the Undugu Society has experienced numerous shifts in both its operational framework and strategies, largely as a result of lessons learned in the course of its development.

Participation in the activities at each of the Youth Centres was not limited to just parking boys. Continous contact with youngsters on the streets and a better understanding of their circumstances caused Undugu to set up a 'reception/drop-in centre' to see to the most immediate needs of this particular category of young people. As the understanding between Father Grol and the boys developed, they were invited to make use of the facilities whenever they needed something to eat or a place to sleep. It was made clear to the boys that using this facility did not obligate them in any way.

As more and more boys took advantage of this reception/drop-in centre Undugu tried to see what it was that caused these boys to live on the streets permanently. Where did they come from? Who and where were their parents? What were their plans and/or thoughts regarding the future? Why were they not in school when the country had already established a system of free primary education?

From the answers, it became clear that most of these boys were children of squatter settlers who, without regular incomes, were often unable to provide even the most basic of their children's needs. Most of the boys had drifted on to the street in search of food, often after being thrown out of school for lack of such things as a regulation uniform or even a pair of shoes. Most boys, when asked, showed a real interest in going back to school, if the opportunity arose. This, it appeared to Father Grol, would be the most logical thing to do, if any measure of rehabilitation and subsequent reintegration into the mainstream of society were to be achieved.

From this point on, attempts were made to place all the youngsters who had expressed an interest in education back into the institutions they had been in.

The overall experience was rather disappointing, most of the schools refusing to readmit the youngsters either because they had missed too much to be able to catch up with their peers or because street life had changed their characters too dramatically for them to fit into a normal school environment. In those few instances where teachers understood and sympathized with the plight of these boys and readmitted them, the boys themselves had major difficulties in fitting back into the regular school routines. Despite the many risks and uncertainties, the children enjoy the freedom of the streets and find it difficult to accept the stricter discipline and monotony of normal school life.

The School for Life

Most street boys, therefore, could not be reabsorbed into the normal school system. Deciding that if these youngsters were to be taught vocational skills, literacy and numeracy were vital, Father Grol organized a loosely structured system to provide them with the basic rudiments of education, 'The School for Life'. A donated church hall was used and classes in basic literacy and numeracy skills were conducted by university students and other volunteers. No demands were made on the learners, other than regular attendance. Some food was provided during the course of the day, however, to compensate for any earnings lost.

The city is indifferent, merciless:
street children – sometimes as young as 5 – lack protection,
intimacy, affection.
Photo: © UNICEF/Francene Keery

The popularity of the School for Life idea grew rapidly as others (both boys and girls) who had been eliminated from the school system got to know about its existence. In the meantime, it became necessary to define the next steps towards re-habilitation for those parking boys about to become literate.

Undugu decided to meet this challenge by establishing an urban variation of the 'village polytechnic'. (The village poly-technic had been a way of training primary-school leavers who could not be absorbed into the secondary-school system and a way of keeping youngsters in the villages.) However, the 'parking boys' had not even received primary education and a more 'informal skills' approach was adopted.

The roots of the problem

As the system for rehabilitating these children evolved, it became clear that, in drawing them off the streets, Undugu was really only addressing the symptoms of a more deeply rooted problem. New boys seemed to replace their peers just as the latter left the street to join Undugu's literacy and numeracy training. Undugu, there-fore, began to interact more with the communities from which these youngsters came. The organization developed a physical presence with field offices in two slum areas and began encoura-ging entire communities to address their development needs to-gether. From this point on, Undugu's growth and diversification concerned the needs and aspirations of these marginalized communities and the challenges that arise from this struggle.

Today, the Undugu Society sees itself as a community development organization focusing on urban poverty issues. The emphasis on working with communities derives from the understanding that the root cause of the street children problem is the poverty that is so glaringly evident in every slum.

Any meaningful attack on this problem must attempt to affect the socio-economic situation of entire communities, rather than to seek to benefit only the few members visible on the streets. A street child, for Undugu, is one that is out of school though of school age. Undugu maintains, therefore, that there are many more hidden and even more vulnerable street children in the slums around the city than meet the eye.

Undugu Society objectives

- To provide basic education and survival skills for street children and out-of-school youths and so increase their potential for employment and self-reliance.
- To enhance the socio-economic status of people in low income areas through an integrated approach to community and small business development.
- To increase the sense of responsibility for their own development among people in low income areas.
- To provide non-financial assistance to other organizations involved in similar activities.
- To reduce progressively the organization's dependence on donor funding to a minimum level.

How Undugu works

During the second half of the 1980s, Undugu underwent a restructuring that focused its operations along three principal themes that define the Nairobi slum communities – organization, employment creation and improvement in the living environment. It now has three programme departments (Community Organization; Employment Creation/Business Development; Production), a Programme Support Department, which undertakes all the organization's research and development activities, and an Administration Department responsible for internal co-ordination and support.

Community Organization Department

The Community Organization Department is responsible for community mobilization and leadership development.

Over 1 million of Nairobi's 2.5 million residents survive as squatters in squalid conditions with no services. Undugu's initial message to communities in slum areas was that the organization wanted to help them improve their living conditions so long as they identified what their priority needs were and had the will to use their innate potential, both as communities and individuals, to address these needs. The Community Organization Department, using development education and leadership training, seeks to stimulate the emergence of a leadership sensitive to the needs of the entire community.

Employment Creation/Business Development Department

High unemployment is the most evident characteristic of almost any slum area. In Kenya there are 600,000 new entrants (both skilled and unskilled) into the labour market each year. In contrast, the formal employment sector creates a little over 50,000 new jobs annually.

The Employment Creation/Business Development Department was set up to focus on basic education, vocational skills and employment – Undugu's 'cycle of employment creation'.

The department is responsible both for the Undugu Basic Education Programme (UBEP), which replaced the School for Life, and for vocational training and apprentice schemes.

Production Department

Working on the hypothesis that, in Kenya, the informal sector will have to absorb the majority of the semi-skilled, unemployed population residing in slum areas, the Production Department represents Undugu's attempt to encourage employment creation in the informal sector through new product development, diversification and marketing.

The Industrial Design Unit in this department develops and tests new products and, after assessing market possibilities, puts them into production. Informal sector artisans are trained in the production of these goods and are encouraged to include them in their own product range.

Administration and Programme Support Departments

Both the Administration and Programme Support Departments play an important role in reinforcing the efforts of the three programme departments. A great deal of continuous experimenting and subsequent enrichment of programme activities takes place to support operations.

In the past, action relating to affordable shelter and necessary improvements in the living environment have been undertaken and refined by the Programme Support Department. This department was responsible for the development of urban agricultural activities in one slum which had a positive and significant impact on both the nutritional status and the economy of the community. It also initiated an extensive public-awareness campaign to inform the Kenyan public of the street children's plight.

Research- and development-oriented, this department brings its capacity and creativity to bear on issues that affect the overall operations of each of the programme departments. Programme support is intended to expand the scope for innovation within the programme departments. Its functional agenda is defined on an on-going basis by the Undugu leadership and draws on the organization's experience with communities.

Footing the bill

Undugu maintains relationships with a wide variety of donors who together provide just over 70 per cent of the organization's total operating funds. The remaining 30 per cent is generated from a range of commercial activities including the operation of a handicrafts shop and an export function for the same products, the manufacture of custom-designed products from the metal and carpentry workshops, and the provision of motor-vehicle services to the open market. Besides generating income for the organization, all Undugu workshops also serve as skills-upgrading units. Over the past two years Undugu has generated some funding from consultancy work undertaken in its area of expertise.

While Undugu has expressed its intention to reduce its dependence on donors, the organization recognizes that the greater part of its current activities related to community building and social welfare could not possibly continue without substantial subsidies from external sources.

The following figures illustrate the scale of the Undugu budget. Total expenditures for the year 1991 amounted to $1.4 million. In 1992, this rose by 15 per cent. These figures include the salaries and expenses of Undugu's 148 full-time staff and 2 voluntary workers seconded to Undugu by international partner agencies.

The cycle of employment creation

Basic education and vocational-skills training have always played a major role in the rehabilitation processes applied by Undugu. It is important to note, however, that these two programmes also form a fundamental part of an employment cycle which, today, is credited with the provision of basic education to just under 4,000 learners and vocational skills to over 2,000 apprentices. These two programmes have also laid the basis for the organization's entrepreneurship initiatives, which have resulted in the setting up of 106 currently operational businesses over the past five years.

Having undergone extensive refinement, the basic education programme has now been granted approval by the Kenyan Government as an acceptable non-formal educational alternative to the formal state-school system. The skills-training apprenticeship system applied by Undugu has also established itself as a viable skills-training approach, since it takes half the time needed by village polytechnics (now called youth polytechnics) to train an apprentice to pass the lowest-grade government trade test.

Most street children have never been to school; or if they have,
they received very little education or education of very poor quality.
Photo: *Dominic Sansoni*

The basic education programme

Under the basic education programme, the Undugu Society operates four basic education centres in the slum areas where most of the learners live. In 1993, the education programme catered for the needs of a total of 581 learners.

The selection of learners is normally carried out by joint teams of teachers and social workers who often have to apply such measures as height-for-age comparisons to ensure that only children over 12 are admitted.

The other determinant that influences the selection of learners is the parents' or guardian's ability to meet the costs associated with the formal school system.

Given that most households in slum districts are single-parent in structure (usually single women), it is often the case that the majority of learners in school have been brought up by a single parent struggling to provide for the learner and other siblings.

The standard family size ranges from five to eight children. In some instances, the learners themselves are required to contribute to the household income by working in jobs such as the collection of waste materials for recycling or even occasionally begging.

Of the 581 learners at present in the programme, 292 are boys and 289 are girls; all are between 12 and 18. About 50 per cent of these learners have attended at least a nursery school and subsequently dropped out.

The general orientation of the basic education programme is towards equipping learners with appropriate skills and sufficient confidence to allow them to face up to the realities of their lives.

It is not uncommon for most learners to be involved in some business activity or other while they attend school. This usually helps supplement the income of the household. In a few instances, such activities are the primary source of income for the household. Where such a situation is known, the learner is encouraged to speak freely about any difficulties experienced, in order that solutions be found inside the school setting.

The curriculum

The Undugu basic education programme has adopted the idea of 'phases' rather than the standards, grades or classes used in the traditional school system. The programme is tiered into three phases, condensing the normal seven years of primary schooling into three years. In Phase 1 (the first year) the learners have their first taste of literacy, numeracy and basic education skills. In Phase 2 (the second year) they develop their capacities in literacy, numeracy and practical work. Phase 3 (the third year) is the final year of the programme. By the end of this phase the learner is expected to have acquired knowledge and proficiency equivalent to that of a child who has completed formal primary education.

These three phases are followed by a year of practical work in which the students can learn skills. These include sheet-metal working, carpentry and tailoring. Each subject takes three months. After nine months of basic skills training, students are expected to select a vocational skill which will become their career. Their training is then completed through the normal apprenticeship system.

Attendance

Besides the demands that are associated with an economically unstable household, regular attendance at these schools is often affected by other factors:

- The teacher's ability to encourage and show due respect to the learners, particularly if they have never been to school before. The challenge is for the teacher to create a sufficiently open environment which encourages learners to articulate their experiences freely.
- For those who may have already attended school and have subsequently dropped out, the main stimulation for attending the programme is curiosity. This becomes a desire to compare the teachers in the programme to those in the state school system.
- The level of attention and recognition accorded to learners is itself a major motivation for continued attendance.

Besides the factors noted above, the most common experience, by far, is that unless the learners have been beset by some apparently insurmountable problem, such as eviction from their slum shelter or, in the case of girls, pregnancy, they are usually keen to complete the three-year educational programme provided at these schools.

When the curriculum used by the programme was being developed, Undugu was able to secure the assistance of the agency responsible for the development of all educational curricula in the country. Thanks to this the curriculum in use is approved as being appropriate for the category of learners attending the Undugu-sponsored schools.

The language commonly used at home and at school is Kiswahili, the national language of Kenya. The curriculum currently includes the following subjects: Kiswahili, English, social studies, Christian religious education, mathematics, science, agriculture, home science, business education, music, art, crafts and physical education.

Learning materials

In view of the need to keep the educational programme as inexpensive as possible, most of the learning materials are acquired from markets within easy reach of the schools. Wherever possible, particularly for subjects such as art and crafts, agriculture, home science, social studies and business education, learners are encouraged to collect learning materials. Learners also do practical work such as running a kiosk as a class business.

The teachers

The basic education programme is run by twenty-six teachers whose ages range from 28 to 50. Ten are women; nineteen attended teacher-training colleges before working with the programme; four have training in the various vocational skills available; and three learned their training skills on the job.

While the curriculum used is fairly specific on what should be taught, the teachers are encouraged to allow sufficient room to accommodate the special interests and concerns of learners in the different subjects.

Participation levels in class are remarkably high, especially in social studies, business education, home science, music, agriculture and all practical work. The students take full responsibility for the care of tools and learning materials. The more knowledgeable learners often guide their peers in the handling of tools they are familiar with. Learners also take full responsibility for the cleaning of classrooms.

Learning assessment

Teachers in the basic education programme use a variety of methods for evaluating the progress in learning: quizzes, continuous assessment and, to a lesser extent, written examinations.

The teachers are expected to apply their creativity in planning their work in accordance with the progress made by learners. The system is not geared to theoretical examinations but rather to self-reliance, and all teaching is conducted in a manner that attempts to create a free-and-easy atmosphere between learner and teacher. Nevertheless, although this basic education programme aims to turn out confident, self-reliant young men and women, those learners who are able to gain entry into the formal education system are encouraged to do so. This is possible for exceptional performers who, on completion of the third phase of the basic education programme, go on to join the fifth year of formal school.

Considering the variety of interests and abilities among learners, teachers often have great difficulty in making the programme sufficiently individualized for each of the learners. Teachers try to identify the learners' special skills or interests and build on them. Those showing a high aptitude for mathematics, for example, are normally given work to suit their ability. Those who are good at making arts and crafts objects are encouraged to show the results of their skills to other learners and teachers, thereby encouraging them to develop their talents further. During the business education lessons, those involved in small businesses are encouraged to tell others about their experiences in business.

Learners who have special problems are provided with individual counselling, often from the teachers. Occasionally, the needs in counselling go beyond the capacity of the teacher and a social worker with the appropriate counselling skills is asked to handle such cases.

Informal skills training

Vocational training at Undugu is geared to give learners skills in various trades. This enables them to become self-employed or be employed in established institutions. The training system is similar to on-job training as practised in the formal sector.

Learners enrolled for vocational training on an apprenticeship basis come under the tutelage of two categories of trainers: working artisans and theory trainers. In 1993, seventy-eight trainees were enrolled for vocational training on an apprenticeship basis and a further twenty were awaiting placement with artisans.

The artisans

Apprenticeship-type instruction is given by local artisans, both male and female, who provide the trainees with practical training. The trainers are all over 25 and most of them have qualifications of Grade 2 level or above.

Those who have not taken any grade tests are already experienced in their trades. They must have been in business for at least five years, running full-time, small-scale businesses. They are paid for the training they give. The period of training differs from trade to trade.

Theory trainers

Classes in the theoretical aspects of each trade are organized for all trainees each Saturday. These are an important component of the training and are intended to motivate the trainees to continue training. At present, Undugu employs six part-time trainers who work for four hours on Saturdays. They have all attained Grade 1 level or higher and some have been through teacher-training colleges. They give theory training and practical demonstrations and prepare trainees for grade tests. They also give business-management training, book-keeping lessons, customer-relations classes and other instruction of use to trainees who start their own businesses. They are difficult to find since Undugu can pay them only 30 Kenyan shillings an hour, a sum which, they say, barely covers their expenses.

Community spirit

Many years have passed since Father Arnold Grol first set foot in Nairobi and, moved with compassion for the swarms of parking boys, set up Undugu in an attempt to alleviate their plight.

From modest beginnings Undugu has grown to become a powerful force fighting to help the street children of Nairobi in their daily battle for survival.

Yet although the basic aims of Undugu – the rescue, rehabilitation and reinsertion of street children into society – remain unchanged, the methods for achieving those aims have been radically transformed. Kenya has a soaring population, nearly half of which is under the age of 14. It is obvious that Undugu, as it was first conceived, cannot possibly cope with this overwhelming onslaught of deprived humanity. The answer, it was decided, lay in stimulating and harnessing the vast potential energies of the poor communities themselves, getting them to define their most pressing needs and stirring them into action.

High unemployment is one of the hallmarks of poor areas. Education in itself is not enough. It has to become a link in the chain of literacy, vocational training and job creation.

The major difficulties for Undugu include the inability of the programme to cope with the large numbers of young people wanting training; the difficulty of rehabilitating young people who have used drugs and find it very hard to cope with a regular programme; and lack of space for training.

On the positive side, Undugu can point with pride to some notable achievements, in particular the successful basic education programme which condenses the normal seven-year period of primary training into three years. At least 2,000 young people have been trained through this programme and now contribute towards the national economy.

Moreover, the first fruits of Undugu's major drive for greater employment opportunities and entrepreneurship are now clearly evident in the 106 operational businesses established over the past five years.

Finally, it should be noted that the success of Undugu's income-generating schemes means the organization will become less reliant upon funds from donors.

Hope for the talibés

The DAARA Association of Malika, Senegal

'Over the years I watched these talibés *begging in the streets or going from house to house. This revolted me, but I told myself that there was nothing I could do. It was a foreign friend who opened my eyes and made me really think about the life these children lead.*'

The struggle against a 'tradition'

The phenomenon of the begging *talibé* (a *talibé* is a pupil of a Koranic school who, in accordance with the Koranic school tradition, begs for his or her living and pays a fee to the marabout or religious instructor) has been a matter of concern to the political and administrative authorities since colonial times.[1]

As long ago as 1896 a decree published by the Governor of the Colony of Senegal and its Dependencies declared: 'Masters in Koranic schools will come to an agreement with the interested parties on the fees to be paid for schooling. They are expressly for-

---

1. The following historical facts are taken from a paper on Arabo-Islamic teaching in Senegal (Islamic Conference, Istanbul, 1985) presented by Professor Mamadou Ndiaye of the University of Dakar.

bidden to send their pupils to collect alms in the streets or by calling at houses.' In order to exercise a certain control over the Koranic schools, to limit the number of marabouts leaving rural areas and to break their hegemony over children's education, the decree included measures which laid down conditions for the exercise of the profession. These stipulated that to run a Koranic school an authorization would first have to be obtained and that the person so authorized had to have been born in Saint-Louis, the capital of the colony, or to have lived there for at least the previous seven years. Finally, the instructors in Koranic schools were placed under the obligation to send their pupils aged 12 to attend a class run by lay teachers or brothers from a Christian order every day.

However, these dispositions, and other similar ones, were insufficient to settle the matter. On the contrary, the phenomenon developed and, after independence, the new Senegal inherited this problem, whose magnitude took on alarming proportions in the context of a social and economic crisis.

On 30 April 1977, at a meeting of the National Council of the Socialist Party, the *talibés* were portrayed as becoming more and more aggressive and, on occasions, maleficent. To put an end to this state of affairs, the Council proposed to give the Koranic schools a status similar to that of private schools.

During the same year, women socialists organized a Senegalese women's study day on the theme of begging and 'human encumbrance'. At the end of this day, they set out proposals for steps to be taken in putting a halt to *talibé* begging. These included progressive reform of teaching methods and a long-term plan which would allow for gradual appropriate legislation to be introduced covering both marabouts and *talibés* as well as obliging *talibés* to wear an identification bracelet on which would be inscri-

The street is also the place where social workers,
'street educators', volunteers, etc., can intervene.
Photo: © UNICEF/Francene Keery

bed the family name, first name and address of both the child and marabout, thereby making identification easier should any offence be committed. At the same time, new legislation forbidding begging (Article 245 of the Penal Code) was adopted, although this included exception clauses which made allowance for alms-collecting of a religious and customary nature.

On 14 July 1977, a restricted Ministerial Council meeting recommended holding a seminar on the *talibé* problem, which would bring together the principal parties.

An opinion poll organized by the Islamic Institute conducted just before the seminar revealed that 55 per cent of those questioned in the Dakar Region found that the *talibés* were a nuisance and 44 per cent thought that the existence of Koranic schools in their present form served no useful purpose. Solutions proposed by those polled included: the creation of modern Koranic schools, the reinsertion of *talibés* into society, the creation of apprenticeship and employment centres for *talibés,* and a ban on begging by *talibés.*

On 17 and 18 May 1978 a seminar on teaching the Koran was held at the Islamic Institute of Dakar. Participants included several traditional Koranic schools, the Ministry of National Education, the Institut Fondamental d'Afrique Noire and the DAARA Association. Three basic recommendations emerged:

1. It is up to the authorities, both religious and governmental, to take all measures necessary for the elimination of begging, juvenile delinquency and so on. Marabouts who exploit *talibés* and thus incite them to begging and to vagrancy will be punished.

2. Parents and schoolmasters must assume their responsibilities with a view to putting an end to this state of affairs which is harmful both to the children and to society.

3. Koranic instruction must be accompanied by professional training so as to enable the *talibé* to assume his responsibilities towards society in the future.

A hostel for *talibés*

'In 1976, faced with this situation, a number of us, including some mothers of varying nationalities, got together and founded the DAARA Association or "hostel" in Arabic.'

The DAARA Association is a private, apolitical, non-denominational, non-profit association whose objective is to fight child begging through the creation of hostels where traditional Islamic instruction is provided for young *talibés*.

The project was founded by a group of mothers and received strong backing from the highest levels of society. In the 1970s, it was one of the first concrete expressions of the new solidarity wave in favour of underprivileged children in urban areas.

'In four years of sustained effort we have achieved our first goal – the creation of a hostel at Malika where talibé *beggar-children living on the streets can be taken in and offered the education that is so vital if they are to become respectable citizens of the future.'*

So, on 14 April 1980, the Association's first hostel, the DAARA of Malika, was opened. The two-hectare site, located 25 kilometres north-east of Dakar, was made available to the Association by the Senegalese Government. The DAARA of Malika is a complex comprising eight dormitories, two playgrounds where classes are held, a general-purpose room, a sick-bay, a kitchen, four staff bedrooms and an administrative office. Over the years, other additions have been made, including a unit for raising chickens, a wind-pump and a carpentry/do-it-yourself workshop. A solar-powered electricity system was installed in November 1990, fifty fruit trees have been planted and a vegetable garden started.

The boarders at the hostel are street children (recruited by the DAARA staff or by other partner members of the associative movement), young people enrolled by their parents and guardians or by the state (Ministry for Women, Children and Family, Ministry of Justice), or children cared for by social workers from the Ministry of Public Health and Social Action.

The majority come from very underprivileged, mainly rural, family backgrounds and a smaller, but still sizeable, proportion come from suburban homes (often single-parent families with the mother and head of the household unemployed, they beg for a living or survive by small-time trading). Children also come from families impoverished by the economic crisis (where the father has lost his job or the job is insecure) or from large families in which the father has retired but only receives a tiny pension. There are a few cases of children of unknown fathers and mentally-ill mothers.

To start with, the DAARA was open, on a voluntary basis, to boys and girls in difficulty or excluded from school, aged 6 to 22. The opening was preceded by an information and public-awareness campaign conducted by the president of the association and the first marabout to be recruited by DAARA. This action received strong support from those who know that this kind of child exploitation is entirely alien to Islam and that, on the contrary, the religion forbids it and calls for solidarity in pre-serving the dignity and interests of children.

The chart drawn up for the new hostel bound the Association to respect the 'Koranic instruction' option. For their part, the parents agreed to accept the Association's pedagogical choices (methods, introduction to other teaching and subject matter) and to give their moral support to their children's education.

Recruitment by 'contact on the ground' was continued until 1983, by which time parents were beginning to come to DAARA of their own accord to request entry for their children. From then on, it was decided that a team consisting of the marabout, the master in charge of the boarders and a social worker or an educational expert should be sent out to inquire into the potential pupil's living conditions. As from 1985 these inquiries were controlled by the director, the marabout, the master in charge of boarders and a sociologist. Admission was ensured if the report bore the inscription '*talibé* in extreme situation'. The age conditions for entry were fixed at a minimum of 5, the age of some of the youngest *talibés* found on the streets, and a maximum of 9. These age limits were adopted in 1985 so as to highlight the plight of the youngest *talibés*. To ensure the project's social integration into the nearby village, the young people of Malika were admitted, but as day pupils only.

'We feel that the virtue of humility can be inculcated in children without obliging them to demean themselves by the bait of gain. Our sole aim is to contribute to making people love and respect that inestimable treasure, the child.'

These young people see the street as a place to make money with odd jobs, a place where chance encounters lead to strong friendships; it is free from social controls and pressures. For these young people, accustomed to surviving on the street in organized autonomous bands, rejecting all authority, school is a useless 'waste of time'. So long as this remains their attitude, getting them back into the social system will be no easy task.

'When something is broken, it has to be repaired!'

DAARA is not a prison. The young people retain the

freedom to agree to become a part of it or not. As for the parents, they have to participate in the children's education by visiting them regularly, receiving them during the holidays and, in one way or another, making a material contribution towards their upkeep. The parent/child relationship is a key criterion for social reinsertion. At present, DAARA has 106 pupils, of whom 66 are boarders and 40 day-pupils from the village of Malika.

The need for innovation

It is generally agreed that the Senegalese education system is in a twofold crisis – a structural dilemma and an identity crisis. Further diagnosis reveals three major deficiencies:

1. A relatively low rate of school enrolment – about 56 per cent according to official sources. There are also great disparities within this rate, with the rural areas coming off the worst.

2. A strong tendency towards marginalization and exclusion during the primary cycle. According to statistics from the Ministry of National Education, out of every 1,000 pupils entering primary school, 300 in rural areas and 200 in urban areas abandon their studies along the way. Furthermore, for several years now, only 10 per cent of those in the secondary cycle get there by passing the competitive examination.

3. The contrast between the education system and the country's needs or identity, and the system's incapability to adapt to the social and economic structural crisis, means that schools are churning out large numbers of people with invalid diplomas. They are hindered rather than helped by the formal curriculum they have pursued and end up swelling the ranks of the unemployed.

Before the present crisis, it was thought that Senegal would attain the objective of free, compulsory schooling for all in 1995/96. Today, some optimistic planners see this target being reached in the middle of the next century. The country cannot sit back and wait for this happy event; it has become urgent to explore other types of informal education capable of satisfying everyone's needs, particularly those of children marginalized by the system.

'Here I am learning French and Arabic. When I grow up I shall be able to run my house and help the poor.'

'DAARA, inspired as it was by the desire to fight the scourge of child begging, an ever-increasing problem in the great urban agglomerations of Senegal, is an example of what is meant by the fundamental right of all children to have a home, to be educated, cared for, practise a religion with dignity and so become complete human beings. These fundamental human values cannot be properly understood unless they are first experienced and lived out in the classroom (the right to speak, the right to information, the right to knowledge, the right to be different, etc.).'[2]

DAARA, from its conception, adopted an educational strategy based on the global education of the child. It respects Senegalese traditions and applies the notion of reciprocal teaching. 'He who knows must teach him who does not' and this holds true in every branch of life. It is the underlying principle of the famous 'child-to-child' method in which the child is both teacher and pupil. This can only be practicable, however, if one begins with a language spoken by all, Wolof, the basic language

---

2. Martine Yahiel, a teacher at the Jules Verne School, Villetaneuse (France), who was the initiator of a project for an exchange between her class and DAARA.

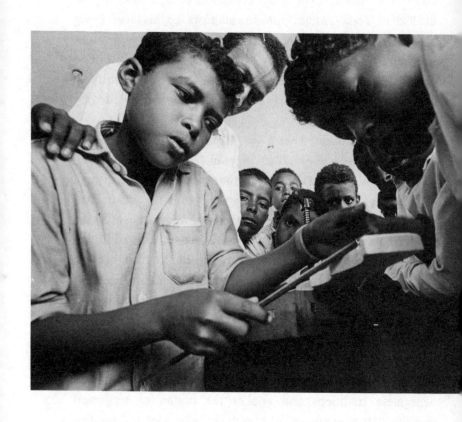

It is essential to restore hope, to eliminate solitude
and safeguard the child's freedom through interactive
and non-coercive education.
Photo: *UNICEF/Werner Muckenhirn*

for literacy training. This is especially true when the target set is a 100 per cent success rate in two years.

Languages and the diversification of activities

The introduction of Wolof teaching has today become one of DAARA's distinguishing features. Some 90 per cent of the boarders devote their first two years to Arabic/Koranic studies and literacy training in Wolof. Wolof is the main language used in horticulture, poultry-raising and carpentry-training. DAARA is also the first school in Senegal to teach productive work and basic environmental education.

With an approach aimed at the humanitarian rehabilitation of marginalized and exploited children, DAARA has led the way in adopting truly concrete measures and solutions. The teaching programme includes Arabic, Wolof, French and mathematics, and the aim is to get pupils up to the official levels required for taking ordinary and competitive examinations. It also includes art, sport and games activities. DAARA's activities have diversified over the years. Alongside the Koranic teaching provided by one (then two) marabouts, agricultural activities have been developed. The garden has expanded with the installation of a wind-pump and ornamental ponds. All the children can now be initiated into gardening.

The length of the teaching cycles varies according to the subject. The Arabic and Koranic studies teaching cycle lasts seven or eight years; French, seven to eight years; Wolof, three to four years; horticulture, four years; poultry-raising, four years; and carpentry, two years; plus six months for bringing pupils up to the normal level.

The two other languages used in teaching are Arabic for the

Arabic/Koranic studies course and French for the French course. In Arabic, the teaching aims to lead the children away from the traditional methods used in Koranic schools. These are based on visual memory and rote learning. The pupils must be able to study the Koran using modern methods and also read and write in Arabic. Since 1985, the most talented pupils have been able to continue their studies in Arabic and go on to take national examinations or enter for competitive examinations.

The teaching of Wolof in Wolof is intended to produce young men and women capable of taking part in the country's development. To give extra value to this education in the mother-tongue, the children carry out inquiries and write about their social, cultural and economic environment.

The objective with French is not quite the same. French is the language of officialdom, and public administration, and the language in which Western-type education is conducted. It gives access to training at the highest level.

The pupils acquire a certain *savoir-faire* which trains them for active life. The courses include initiation into environmental management, the growing of cereals (millet, maize, etc.), horticulture and small-scale rearing of domestic animals.

To make DAARA self-suffcent and profitable, poultry-raising activities were intensified in 1984 and, in 1985, market-gardening activities were brought up to a more commercial level. At the same time, classes on the socio-economic climate and the techniques of conservation and ecological transformation were being developed. In 1984, the pupils took part in the national reforestation campaign and learnt about the value of the various species of tree.

Elementary carpentry and masonry also form part of this 'apprenticeship for active life'. This has the double advantage of contributing to the upkeep of the premises and encouraging the pupils to go on to learn these trades. Since 1990, woodwork and metalwork have been part of the curriculum.

DAARA has adopted the formal education sector's system of monthly assessment and half-yearly examinations (starting in the middle of the primary cycle) for Arabic and French. In Wolof, tests are linked to the end of the cycle and to the national competitive examination organized by the directorate of literacy training and basic education. For environmental education, evaluation is made on a group basis and according to activity. Technical and/or professional training is evaluated according to the items produced, management skills and theoretical knowledge. In horticulture and poultry-raising there are three evaluation phases.

Proficiency certificates are not awarded – the main goal of the teaching being to enable the pupils to learn to read and write in French or Arabic and (inevitably) in Wolof. The system established at Malika is oriented more towards practical training so that, their studies completed, the pupils will become prime movers of development. Some 10 per cent of pupils have gone in for national and competitive examinations, in particular those for entry to secondary education. Four former pupils are now completing the final year at a state secondary school. Another is in his second year at a technical *lycée* and seven others are attending private secondary schools. Three pupils have successfully taken the examinations for the horticultural training centres run by the Ministry of Labour and Professional Training. One has obtained a *Certificat d'aptitude professionnelle,* another is at present in charge of DAARA's horticultural programme and the third has set up in business on his own.

An open education system in open surroundings

The education system developed in DAARA combines the requirements of general education and those of the individual placed within a specific social and group context. These groups play an active part in the shaping and development of the milieu where the individual is evolving. Accordingly, the pedagogical system adopted is relatively open, active and adaptable. It centres on the immediate, endogenous milieu, emphasizing basic elements such as reading, writing and arithmetic, while at the same time encouraging artistic and cultural creativity. The institutional framework is not limited to the classroom; it includes the courtyard, the market-garden complex, the playing-fields, the carpentry workshop and the village area. It does not rely solely upon the teaching staff; anyone who has special knowledge of the 'whys' and 'hows' of life may be called upon to share his or her wisdom with the pupils. Public memory workshops involving activities based on traditional stories, as well as other forms of creative workshops, are held on Wednesdays and during free time. The children have access to pottery, modelling, theatre and painting, and all kinds of sport (football, badminton and table tennis for instance).

Except for a few children brought along by employees of the Ministry of Justice or by social workers from the Ministry of Public Health and Social Action, all boarders follow courses regularly.

The staff consists of a director, a supervisor to teach French and mathematics, two teachers for Arabic and the Koran, a teacher for French and Arabic, a Wolof teacher, three women in charge of the kitchen, linen and cleaning plus a night watchman.

The programme allows for 'catching-up' classes. Individualized orientation or advice meetings are held at the start of term or during the year.

The pedagogical council normally meets once a month but can be convened at the request of any member. It makes proposals concerning the students' progress and pupils, parents or guardians have the right to be heard.

The older pupils join in the decisions concerning the educational, technical and professional training programmes and participate in the upkeep of installations. Two democratically elected pupil representatives attend the pedagogical council. In the classrooms, even the youngest pupils are in charge of teaching materials, and the poultry-raising or market-gardening groups are responsible for the upkeep of their equipment.

Social and economic reinsertion

In 1987, DAARA and various non-governmental organizations and national associations founded an Action and Solidarity Group to help underprivileged urban areas. This Group, created out of a desire for solidarity, aims to encourage joint programmes for children.

The Group's first venture was a reforestation camp or 'worksite/school' at the Malika DAARA. The camp lasted three weeks and included joint activities such as tree planting or manual work. The project reached about a hundred children under the supervision of some twenty leaders and ten instructors, all of whom were volunteers.

In the attempt to find further solutions and create a new partnership and strategy in the fight to help child beggars, a working group has been formed which comprises the Islamic Institute of Dakar, ENDA Tiers Monde, ATD Quart Monde, the Ministry in charge of women's and children's welfare, UNICEF and DAARA at Malika.

Finally, DAARA aims to establish a follow-up sector that would maintain contact with young people in apprenticeships up to the time when they are successfully reinserted into society. A partnership with youth associations for development and non-governmental organizations specialized in the training and reinsertion of deprived young people into society is the chosen option.

DAARA's attempts to place young people in large businesses have rarely met with success. There have also been experiments in setting them up in small businesses by granting loans to restricted groups. Experiments in limited-scale trading of foodstuffs have been no more successful. Great difficulties are being encountered in this area. Some 10 per cent of the young people come back after training and ask for help in finding employment, especially when they want to work on their own. At the moment, DAARA encourages them to organize themselves in groups with similar economic interests. It then helps them search for funds once they have a scheme drawn up or a project formulated.

The need for general mobilization

'One day, I saw a boy begging at some traffic lights in Dakar. I had 120 francs for my bus fare so I gave him 10 francs, saying to myself that it would just mean that I would have to walk a little bit farther. It was at DAARA that I learned to have the courage to go up to a

child. Before, it used not to bother me to see a talibé *in the street; now, it hurts me.'*

'That little "extra" that we have, compared with our fellow pupils, is, first, that we have mastered our mother-tongue, which we can read and write and, second, we have been through an education system which has given us the feeling that we know how to do something.

'If we don't find work, we will all be able, later on, to raise chickens or become farmers.'

All the pupils in apprenticeships with artisans would agree with the following words of one of their number:

'I am the only apprentice who knows how to read and write and draw diagrams. When the boss explains something, I note down what he has said in Wolof. From time to time I make notes in Arabic or French. This is my way of staying in contact with these languages.'

Some of these pupils do, in fact, come back to DAARA with their notebooks and ask the Arabic or French teachers to point out any mistakes they have made.

Can the experiment of the DAARA at Malika be considered a success? Can it be held up as a model in the context of education for all?

Before these questions can be answered, we have to look again at what is at stake, not only in terms of the objectives determined at the beginning, but also in terms of the national context.

The programme's objective was to eliminate institutionalized begging which forced children from 4 to 14 to bring money and other gifts to their marabouts. If the project was to be credible, it had to result in obvious social and educational success – rehabilitation and reinsertion into society, on the one hand, and the creation of a new pedagogy and educational model on the other.

Contacts with local leaders, marabouts and parents, however, need to be multiplied in order to formulate a better kind of education. What is needed is a system to teach all children to read, write and have access to professional training and, above all, a way for young people to take part in the national effort for development.

The path for the years to come involves the mobilization of all skills, in a partnership with other agencies with similar concerns. This would lead to a real sharing of knowledge and experience. It would involve both the public and religious authorities as well as a vast media operation aimed at raising general public awareness and mobilizing its support.

But there is a long way to go before ambitions are translated into achievements, as is seen in the failure of a considerable number of young people hoping to achieve economic reinsertion. Many obstacles remain. Community participation will have to be maintained. Other difficulties include the lack of appropriate teaching materials and the impossibility of providing the teaching staff with better-adapted training.

Given the results obtained during the first decade of its existence as a pilot project, the balance-sheet can only be described as positive.

Surviving
in the streets
at 4,000 metres

ENDA-Bolivia Project, El Alto, Bolivia

At the World Congress of the United Towns Organization, held in Lima, Peru, in 1987, the Bolivian town of El Alto, 10 km to the east of the capital, La Paz, was awarded, given the average age of its population, the title of youngest town in Latin America. Unfortunately, it was also awarded another title – that of the continent's poorest town.

There is something extreme and unique about the town's situation. The traveller landing at the airport sees a semi-desert steppe, the puna or high plateau of the Andes, stretching for hundreds of kilometres all around, and beyond, as far as the eye can see, the breathtaking mountain scenery of the Cordilleras. But the 450,000 who live in El Alto have very different concerns. In 1988:

- practically 80 per cent of the built-up areas were without public lighting;
- only three in ten of the inhabitants had piped drinking water in their homes;
- there were only 4 km of paved streets;
- there was only one doctor per 10,000 inhabitants, one thirty-bed hospital for the entire population, three medical centres, eighteen public first-aid posts, and roughly fifty private medical services;

- the infant mortality rate of 300 deaths per 1,000 births was the highest in all Latin America.

The very specific geographical conditions of the Altiplano, which towers up to an altitude of 4,000 metres, also raise specific problems of human survival because of the permanent cold and the need for physiological adaptation. Those who have absolutely nothing are, therefore, highly tempted to take drugs in varied forms.

In 1987, Michel Grégoire discovered the plight of El Alto's street youngsters and children. On his initiative, on 1 January 1988, ENDA-Bolivia, a non-governmental organization, was set up with a dual aim: to help actual and potential street children escape from drug abuse and to create conditions favourable for their re-entry into community life.

This chapter looks at the results of five years' relentless effort, made possible through the co-operation of numerous national and international institutions – the Bolivian Committee for Solidarity and Social Development (JNSDS), the National Board for the Struggle Against Drug Use (DINAPRE), the United Nations Children's Fund (UNICEF) and the United Nations Fund for Drug-abuse Control. The agreement reached with the two Bolivian institutions enabled the organization's initial experiment on the Altiplano – the Integral Prevention Programme for High-Risk Juvenile and Marginalized Populations – to be extended to Amazonia, where it is working with young Indians in urban areas, and the Beni District. However, we will concentrate here on the experience acquired in El Alto.

Children in the street, children of the street

The present population of El Alto consists mostly of recent migrants of rural origin; the majority are Aymara Indians. The city's ethnic make-up remains a mosaic, however, with people from all parts of Bolivia, including the high Andean plateaux, the Amazon, the central valleys, the lowlands and the Chaco. The school-age population of El Alto alone accounts for 55 per cent of the population, although there are only fifty-six state and twenty-one private schools. The dilapidated condition of the city's educational facilities and services greatly contributes to the drop-out rate and to the presence of young people on the streets. The town has about 50,000 children and adolescents – 11 per cent of the population – who can be described as 'living in the street', that is who spend more than 75 per cent of their time in the street, at any rate during daytime, although they generally return home at night. There are also 3,000 street children, children who have no homes at all (less than 1 per cent of a total population of 450,000). Throughout the country as a whole, it is estimated that there are 80,000 working children under 14, and more than 20,000 who have to fend entirely for themselves.

For this very reason the programme is particularly aimed at working children and adolescents – street vendors, shoeshine boys or employees in small shops or stores – children who often work more than twelve hours a day for an average wage of $2, or some $60 a month. As in so many other Third World countries, the resources available to the government departments are inadequate when compared with the needs. The role of such organizations as ENDA-Bolivia is essential. Above all, steps have to be taken to prevent children, who have to struggle against exhaustion and sometimes against cold and hunger, from sinking into the world of drugs, in particular 'poor man's drugs' – such as solvents, glues or fuels. Some 80 per cent of the children or adolescents concerned confess to having, at one time or another, sniffed substances of this kind.

This precocious entry into the labour force (and in such conditions!) is not a matter of choice. Most often it is an absolute necessity. In Bolivia, the average age for starting work is 10 but it can be as low as 6, sometimes even 5. What can be the meaning of the word 'education' in such a context? Priorities here are clear to see. What has to be done is to prevent working children 'who live in the street' from becoming 'street children', and to save other children from the street.

It is important to grasp the distinction made, within this programme, between 'children of the street' and 'street children'. In both cases, of course, we are dealing with children whose lives are spent essentially in the literally 'physical', but also economic, area of the street. The difference between the two is nevertheless considerable.

The child 'in the street' is one who plays, roams, or works in the street but who has not broken off all ties with his or her family, community or neighbours. In most cases, the child joins in certain school activities, even if school attendance is not regular. How, then, does he or she become a 'street child'? If the child has recently arrived in the city, he or she will, at first, have preserved some links with the rural community and so be steeped in certain cultural values. The child is, nevertheless, going to be left to his or her own devices for a time by the parents, who return to the country for seasonal events such as harvests, sowing time, or traditional ceremonies. All too soon, then, this child will abandon the road to school and discover the world of the street.

Another even more powerful factor is going to keep the child there. In Bolivia, a child 'in the street' is a child who works – sometimes from the age of 5 or 6. In general, children will have been pushed to work by the parents, themselves faced with insurmountable economic problems. The child's work is often, both for the youngster and for his or her family, a simple issue of survival, and the street is the only place of work which society offers. Food, clothing and a minimum amount of hygiene and health care: all these will depend on the child's capacity to survive in such an environment. All too soon, the child may even be bringing home more money than the parents, and will be coming home later and later. The child will then be discovering a kind of street 'family' that will, sometimes, appear, at least for a spell, to be more welcoming than his or her own. There will come the day when the child will think that he or she might as well keep the day's money and not come home at all. At this point, the child 'in the street' has become a 'street child'.

The child 'in the street', albeit in difficulty, has parents and belongs to a community. For the 'street child', however, the 'cultural' setting of the street (with its customs, attitudes and values) becomes the permanent setting of life. Such a child has lost all community and family ties, and has made the street the one and only environment. Not only does the youngster play, wander, or even work in the street but also eats and sleeps in it, partaking of all the 'dubious pleasures' this world has to offer. In particular, there is the constant reality of drugs. It should not, however, be thought that a child like this entertains illusions about the street 'family' for long, or about the fellowship of the 'wretched'. Street life is in fact made up of latent or open violence, of selfishness, and solitude. The child will want to escape and has to be helped to do so.

In El Alto, as noted, there is a difference in size between the two groups concerned, there being some 50,000 'children in the street' and about 3,000 'street children'. Consequently, while a recovery effort must be undertaken for some, what is needed for the majority is an enormous labour of prevention. It should not be thought that a child 'in the street', who is in a clearly abnormal high-risk situation, is already a delinquent and still less a drug addict. A child who takes drugs on a habitual basis cannot be, at the same time, a child who works in the street since the never-ending tasks and chores, and the constant effort would be too great.

These, then, are the considerations which, from the outset, have guided the activities of ENDA-Bolivia's prevention programme.

ENDA-Bolivia's resources

To begin with, the organization consists of a staff of professional educators, psychologists and social workers, a legal adviser, an administrator and an accountant. All in all, there are some seventy persons in El Alto and in the Beni District. The founder, Michel Grégoire, is currently responsible for international co-ordination.

The organization has eleven centres. In El Alto, there are two hostels (the House of Brotherhood and the Casa Qantuta), one community home (the Casa Minka) and four production units – a small factory for bricks or cement slabs (the Casa Yanapacuna), a unit for reprocessing solid waste (the Casa Qumanani), a farm (the Casa Waki) on the outskirts of El Alto and a unit for making educational wooden toys. In addition, there are two more hostels in the Beni District and in Amazonia (the Casa Tamarindo in Trinidad and the Casa Mamore in

*Only education can arm the marginalized child
against the vicious circle of ignorance
and the inability to control one's own destiny.*
Photo: *UNESCO/F. Caracciolo-Fay Banoun*

Guayamerin), and three production units (a pottery workshop, a moped maintenance workshop, and a farm).

ENDA-Bolivia's financial resources are based on funds (such as grants and subsidies) from the following sources: multilateral assistance (the United Nations, the European Commission, the Red Cross, the Organization of American States); bilateral assistance (European governments, the United States, Canada, Bolivia); grants from private Western and Bolivian organizations which fund development projects; and local solidarity networks (aid groups, friends, parents).

It is estimated that 3,500 children or adolescents have, at one time or another, profited from the programme since its foundation.

The Integral Prevention Programme: three fundamental targets, six strategies for intervention

ENDA-Bolivia's activities have, from the start, been aimed at three fundamental targets: (a) to reduce the amount of time spent by minors in the street; (b) to bring about favourable conditions for their reintegration into the community; and (c) to improve the manner of their socialization. Reaching these targets has meant applying six strategies, each involving a specific field: research, communication, participation in management, services, job resources and training.

These objectives are ambitious, but they also aim to be realistic. It is obvious that the street cannot be an environment where, in the long run, a child can develop in a positive way. On the other hand, the reality is there to be seen – given Bolivia's current economic and social conditions, it is impossible to tear children completely away from the streets. One can only reduce the amount of time they spend there and take advantage of this time gained to further their education and subsequent reintegration into society by making use of non-formal teaching and innovative methods of alternative instruction. Similarly, while the ideal, of course, would be to give these children a new family, or to restore them to the family they have lost, the initial objective remains more modest – to integrate them into a community, and into a material and social environment where their personalities can develop harmoniously. Reaching the third target – where the issue is the relation between child and society – involves a change of attitudes on both sides. The child must change his or her own views of course, since the point is to encourage reintegration; but society at large, which has to understand its responsibility in the children's plight, must change its attitude also. It is all the more unjust to show prejudice, hostility and scorn towards such children.

Attaining all three of ENDA-Bolivia's targets means implementing six strategies. The first strategy involves research. Before programming its anti-drug campaign, the staff carried out a survey in El Alto, with thousands of interviews among the most varied sectors of the population such as youth gangs, mothers, teachers, etc.

The second strategy encourages communication at all levels through regular meetings, workshops and appropriate use of audiovisual material. Educational electronic games are used a lot. 'Children of the street' and 'street children' are, unfortunately, much attracted by electronic amusement arcades (known in Bolivia as *tilines*), where the dominant themes are violence, sex and money. They often end up spending the better part of their scant resources there. This explains the relative importance accorded to educational electronic games – they allow the children's interest in this sort of game to be channelled into educational purposes.

Children who have always been rejected or ignored must be made to feel, in practical terms, that they are in a position, at long last, to take part in the shaping of their own future, instead of being the resigned instruments of their own destruction. Such a youngster must, therefore, also be able to help define the educational and teaching programme, join in the various professional and technical activities, and even lend a hand in the administration and funding. This is the intention behind the third strategy – participation in management.

A practical example of this is the creation of micro-co-operatives, tiny businesses adapted to the experience of working children. The management of these little 'youth stores' – which stock various items such as shoe polish, toothbrushes and school stationery – is entirely in these youngsters' hands. They themselves directly handle all matters to do with stocking the store, dealing with the suppliers, and so on.

The fourth strategy involves the offer of services of all kinds ranging from food, hygiene and teaching to social, medical, technical or legal. Services may also concern more specific matters, even things which might appear as mere details at first sight, but whose importance is much greater than one might think. Take the example of lockers. These lockers, with a key to lock them, are made available to the children and in fact meet two needs, one practical and one psychological. The brotherhood of the street world is only a sham and no working child can afford to lose sight, for even a moment, of any valuable objects (shoeshine kit, for example) or else things risk being stolen. In such a constant frame of mind, the child can hardly be expected to devote all his attention to the activities at the centre.

Once the children have their own locker and key, however, they find themselves free, at last, of one of the major daily worries. Nor is this all, for there enters into the picture one further element fully as meaningful as the practical aspect. Giving an individual locker to a street child is of the greatest psychological importance. It is an event. For the first time perhaps, they have of 'their own', a place where a few meagre things can be kept. At last there is a 'private space'.

The programme also attempts to give the children the material means of escaping from the 'culture of the street', through a fifth strategy of providing job resources. This strategy offers the children the opportunity of joining one of the micro-businesses, where they are able to assume management responsibilities, acquire technical skills and learn to participate in a collective form of activity while preparing in the meantime for going to school. On joining, the child or adolescent pledges to keep the following three rules: (a) to work as a member of a team; (b) to carry out what is necessary to return to the school system, with the permanent help of the programme's educational specialist; and (c) to learn to manage a personal budget properly by making use of the savings system designed by the programme. The child will therefore be working on a part-time basis (in the morning or evening), while the other half of usual working time will be spent in preparing for reintegration into school. It has been calculated that it would have taken such a child fourteen days to earn, in the street, what he is guaranteed to make in only one day in a 'micro-business'. The strategy offers the child an authentic alternative, from an essential point of view – that of survival.

These micro-businesses are active in the most varied fields, from preserving the environment (reprocessing waste) and contributing to urban development (manufacturing bricks and cement slabs), to support for handicrafts (with shops selling hand-crafted cards) and informal education (by means of workshops manufacturing educational wooden toys). The Centro de Producción de Losetas ENBOL, for example, employs thirty youngsters, all of them former street children, aged 15 to 18, who manufacture small cement slabs or bricks to serve many different purposes. One of the main markets for these is the paving of El Alto's streets. The workshop's educational wooden toys are sold to various teaching centres and the demand for them is on the increase to the point that their export is being considered, through commercial bodies which support initiatives of this sort in the Third World. Work on the toys currently involves twenty-two youngsters, aged 17 to 25.

All these activities amount to a global strategy for prevention, assistance and reintegration, carried out daily in the programme's different hostels. More than 500 children and adolescents – aged 7 to 18 – pass through these hostels each day or more sporadically. All children can use the cafeteria, showers, laundry, dispensary, individual or family-oriented psychological guidance service and legal assistance service, and have the possibility of enjoying various educational or recreational activities (a library, video, and computer, a collection of games, drama, dancing and music). Since the most deprived and their basic needs should certainly not be forgotten, a dormitory has been opened, in co-operation with the Bolivian authorities, to provide temporary shelter to those children who usually sleep out in the cold – at a temperature of minus 10 degrees Celsius – under cardboard sheets or newspapers in the public parks.

The future

The consistency and remarkable continuity of ENDA-Bolivia's objectives and strategy should not, however, lead one to believe that there is any room for the slightest spirit of routine. This is a living programme, and each year brings its harvest of initiatives and innovations. Among the most recent, was the creation in 1991, in co-operation with JNSDS (the Bolivian public organization responsible for the protection of working minors), of the Casa Qantuta, as the headquarters of a project dealing specifically with the plight of young girls in high-risk situations.

In this respect, it should be borne in mind that, in El Alto:

- the average life expectancy for women is 46;
- girls generally work in the 'non-formal' commercial sector so they have no social protection;
- seven out of every ten illiterates are women;
- more than 40 per cent of child workers are girls, with an average age of 11 to 14 years;
- only 32 per cent of these girls, whether children or adolescents, regularly attend school.

Projects are not lacking for the next five years. Without a doubt, the most ambitious of these will be the creation of an International Centre for the Training of Street Educators (CERFOCAL), with the support of various international organizations, including UNESCO and the Commission of the European Communities.

Piranhas and dolphins

CEDRO Project, Lima, Peru

Lima is one of those enormous Third World urban sprawls to which the name 'city' is still applied out of force of habit. Millions of people, from all parts of the country, have come here in search of a better life for themselves and for their children – and in most cases in vain. Out of a population of nearly 7 million, up from less than 700,000 only a half-century ago, how many homeless children now roam the streets? There are thousands in Lima itself, according to some sources, and even more, according to other sources, throughout the country's other cities. Statistics do not seem very reliable and depend on the meaning given to the term 'street child'. In the strict sense, it applies to children who lack any sort of family or social framework.

Where do these children come from? In nine out of ten cases, they belong to the second generation of families of rural origin. Some 50 per cent have lived in families where one of the two parents was either not their biological father or not their biological mother; 90 per cent of those questioned by the programme's organizers complained of having been beaten at home. Many are not abandoned children but rather children who have run away from ill-treatment. Habitually, these youngsters are referred to as children. They are, though, most often adolescents or pre-adolescents. According to the programme organizers' own surveys, some 70 per cent of Lima's street children are aged 12 to 14 and the rest aged from 7 to 11 or 15 to 17.

From October to December 1988, the Lima street-children programme co-ordinator Dwight Ordóñez, working on behalf of the Centro de Información y Educación para la Prevención del Abuso de Drogas (CEDRO, a Peruvian non-governmental organization combating drug use since 1986) carried out a preliminary survey of conditions in the city in view of taking potential measures and action. His work made it possible in early 1989 to lay down broad guidelines for a programme and for negotiations to start with the authorities in the hope of obtaining premises. An initial team of educators was put together in mid-1989 and the first contacts with children were systematically begun in September in the centre of Lima and in the Miraflores district, areas with two of the highest concentrations of street children in the city.

Two homes were opened in May 1990 in Miraflores and central Lima, with a total capacity of about fifty places. In January 1991, the team began street work in two other critical sectors – the port zone of Callao, and the area around La Parada–La Victoria, the city's main area for delinquency and drug-addiction. In February 1992, work finally started with street girls. The Callao home (thirty-two places) opened in July 1992.

By November 1992, the programme had five homes, four for boys and one for girls, all located in those four areas of Lima where the problem seems to be most acute. Total capacity was 144 beds, with an almost 80 per cent rate of occupancy (central Lima, 32; La Victoria–La Parada, 32; Miraflores, 24; Callao Port, 32; the home for girls in central Lima, 24).

Education must give street children
the basic learning tools and awaken their potential.
Photo: *UNICEF/Shamsuz Zaman*

At the time of writing, the project had a staff of forty-three: the co-ordinator, twelve staff responsible for tasks of a general nature (administration, secretariat and so forth), twenty-five street educators (five to each home) and a full-time social worker for each home. The latter sees to the youngsters' return to school and families, and also to their medical check-ups. Volunteer assistants and those following courses in social work also find their particular slot in the project, as do the heads of the vocational training workshops already in place.

Funds for the programme come from various sources. Main donors include the European Union ($136,000 in 1990–92), whose assistance enabled the project to be launched; CARITAS-Netherlands ($90,000 in 1992); and various institutions in the United States ($235,000 in 1991/92) and the United Kingdom ($25,000 in 1991, but $320,000 earmarked for 1992–94). The programme receives no direct assistance from the Peruvian Government.

'Open' homes

We have seen how those responsible for the programme have chosen to deal, at least initially, not with working children or with children 'in' the street in general, but with children 'of' the street in the strict sense, that is, those children who have broken all family ties, who have no economic activity, formal or informal (as street vendors or the like), but who survive only by illegal means (theft, etc.), take drugs, and live in gangs by night. These gangs, though, are small, highly mobile groups and difficult to make contact with.

Night work therefore is essential and carried out by the street educators several times a week. Any opening of a home is preceded by several months of intensive work. Each home, in fact, was the result of an agreement between the educators and those street children, already motivated enough to enter, who reached a joint decision and negotiated rules for living together, in common. These fundamental rules, in turn, amounted to a consciously accepted break with the laws of the street 'sub-culture' – so no drugs, no sex, no theft, no violence, but instead, participation on an egalitarian basis in all the activities of the community. Failure to observe these rules may result in sanctions that can even include temporary exclusion, decided on collectively by both children and adults.

Project organizers believe that since the children live in groups, positive use of the peer pressure exerted by the group should be made. In the street world, such pressure is harmful, making drug use almost mandatory, but here it can also create and impose a counter-culture, a reverse image of the street.

The homes are constantly receiving so-called unstable children (those whose permanent stay lasts less than a month). They represent between 10 and 40 per cent of the total number in each home. There is a considerable danger that these children from outside might try to introduce drugs and negative influences among those children who are stable (that is, those who have been in the homes for several months). This is a problem which the organizers choose to face because it is inseparable from the very philosophy underlying their project, namely, that traditional 'closed' institutions are unable to train individuals capable of dealing with any social life. Whatever the attendant difficulties, the children must develop as far as possible in conditions which are statistically and socially 'normal' and not protected, artificial or special. A home should not be an aquarium, nor should the 'piranhas' (the name that the children actually give themselves) feel cooped up in it – otherwise they might yield to the temptation of running away for good. Instead, the children must be given the chance to become truly socialized individuals, or 'dolphins'. The children in all these homes are familiar with the image, and so can recognize the positive metamorphosis that it represents. The dolphin has become the symbol of the project.

In addition, the possibility of influencing others also works the other way and the world of the home may, in turn, destabilize that of the street. Particular importance is attached here to the project's drug programme. Nearly 100 per cent of all street children have taken drugs at one time or another (usually glue-sniffing). Twice a week, programme organizers arrange workshop sessions – with videos followed by a discussion and occasional role-playing. This enables the children to understand and see the true consequences of drug abuse on health and personality.

The project's notion of an 'open house' policy also carries another meaning, for if the doors to the homes are always open, this is also to enable the children and adolescents to rejoin society (their families and work) as quickly as possible. The project must be a passage-way where new recruits can be continuously welcomed. Above all, the project organizers must not yield to the temptation of re-creating a closed system, putting off the moment when the youngsters ought to be leaving. The project tries to avoid setting goals that are too ambitious or burdening the project with tasks that do not form part of its purpose. The ideal would be to limit, to about ten months, the duration of each child's stay in a home. These months should be devoted to preparing the youngsters for going to school or back to their families or, in the case of adolescents, starting work.

Going to school

One needs to bear in mind that a child fresh off the street will, potentially, be the poorest student that one can imagine. For the word 'education' to mean anything for such a child, one must first set about structuring his life and behaviour by getting him to accept the basic standards governing the life of the home. Until this process of re-socialization has been concluded (and this can take some three months), all efforts at instruction will be useless. On average, these children usually lag two or three years behind the school level normally corresponding to their age. The project has no special educational facilities or programme and the children go to the nearest state school. Nevertheless, before sending them to school, an effort must be made to bring the children up to the right level and get them accustomed to schoolwork. If they so wish, the children can have an average of two hours a day personal basic instruction in reading, writing and arithmetic.

The problem of educating these children is all the greater because they rely on others. Slowness, lack of motivation, a short attention span and the like may be their problem, but there is the other problem of enrolment, which is not always an easy matter. Generally speaking, these children have no birth certificates – nor indeed any identity papers – and can provide no proof of previous schooling even when they happen to have had some. Enrolling children, in time, can become a bureaucratic problem.

Even when enrolled, however, such children are not always made very welcome. The office staff, teachers or other students sometimes shun them, which may cause them to drop out after a short period. The project organizers, for this reason, prepare leaflets for distribution to the teachers in order to make them aware of the specific problems these children face, what attitudes and words to avoid, and so on. In addition, since the teaching methods of some of these instructors are based almost entirely on pure rote learning, already discouraging for the other children, they have an absolutely catastrophic effect on former street children.

A programme to keep them busy

While it is certainly vital to give children a roof, a bed and food, and provide them with medical care and psychological aid, it is no less necessary to prepare them for school or vocational training. Nevertheless, between meeting basic needs and undertaking first training, there is a further, essential link if these children are to be sufficiently motivated to give up street life. This consists of a wide range of recreational activities and sports, and various manual activities. One cannot lay enough stress on the importance of these activities in providing a psychological structure for these children and adolescents.

Facilities therefore exist in a number of homes so that the children can play soccer, basketball, volley-ball, ping-pong or table football. Contests are regularly arranged between teams from the different homes. All the homes have television and video, and several of them have painting studios. One home even has a music studio where children can learn to play the *quena* (flute) and other native Peruvian instruments.

In each home, every day or every other day, at least two hours are devoted to various manual activities that the children can choose from, although they have to do at least one. The programme organizers have noted that these activities have had remarkably good effects on the children's behaviour and that not joining in could cause some children to lapse back into forms of behaviour which it had been thought they had outgrown (violence, theft). There are workshops producing a great variety of things – bracelets, embroidered cloths, silk-screen prints, furry toys and the like – which are sold either at exhibitions periodically organized by the programme or from the mushroom-shaped stalls or booths described below.

Preparing for work

This is one aspect of the programme which is more difficult for the organizers to assess. Except in one case, the workshops, with vocational training for those aged over 14, the essential aim is to prevent the older adolescents, who ought not to stay too long in the homes, from lapsing back into delinquency for lack of means. The programme therefore tries to give them some useful vocational training and at the same time integrate them into a real economic circuit where they will be able to establish an immediate link between their work and earnings by offering the sale of their goods and services.

In the Callao home there is a joinery workshop, a machinery workshop and a broom-making workshop. There is another, for printed cloth, at the home in central Lima and three more at the home for girls, for machine sewing, pottery and knitwear. Two more workshops are being set up – a bakery in La Victoria and a workshop for making canvas shoes in Miraflores.

The programme also attempts to place adolescents directly in small businesses, shops and so on, but this is difficult as there is much reluctance to be overcome on both sides. The educators need to keep a close eye on these young people if the experiment is to succeed. Just as in the case of schools, the project distributes explanatory brochures to employers, concerning words and attitudes to be avoided at all costs.

The programme has also introduced sales-booths, stalls shaped like large, coloured mushrooms, leased out to traders on condition that they employ – on a part-time basis – one of the project's young people (aged 13 to 14). About twenty such booths are in operation now, but keeping a former street child for more than four hours in the same place is no easy task.

Vocational training presents the organizers with two specific problems. Firstly, the Peruvian authorities do not yet officially recognize the training programme, so there is no certificate to validate it. Secondly, the children themselves suffer from their own very different psychological problems. The feelings they entertain about training and work are highly mixed. They are very motivated in so far as they know the cost of things and the living conditions in Peru. At the same time, what these children have rediscovered on entering the homes is their childhood. So what they really prefer to do is play. It is, then, much harder for them to rid themselves of the idea that the programme is trying 'to make them leave' when it is suggested they return to the outside world. This is a feeling which it is difficult for them to express and can result in problems.

Rejoining the family

It is rare for a child to have lost all contact with his or her family. A permanent effort to restore children to their families is, therefore, made by staff members, under the responsibility of a social worker assigned to each home and assisted by psychology trainees. This is a particularly onerous task, calling for frequent travel, often on Sundays and occasionally in high-risk sectors. It calls for a great listening capacity and negotiation skills to find out each version of the facts. Gradually an effort is made to modify attitudes and overcome reluctance. Results so far have not been insignificant – 45 per cent of the stable children have rejoined a family environment (which does not necessarily mean a nuclear family). In about two-thirds of these cases, results have so far been favourable. Where rejoining the family has been a failure, one in three children has rapidly returned to one of the project's homes instead of going back to the street.

Results and plans

The programme's results are satisfying, at least in relation to the population concerned. As of June 1992, it could be reasonably estimated that the project's educators had managed to make contact with all the youngsters in the four areas where Lima's street children seem to be concentrated. Nearly 90 per cent of these children have spent some time in one of the project's homes. It has been possible to get roughly 25 per cent of the project's children to rejoin their families. Some 30 per cent were visiting their families at weekends and a similar percentage were going to school.

This is why, over the next two years, and following the successful pattern set in Lima, CEDRO is going to try to set up similar programmes in six other Peruvian cities – Cuzco, Huancayo, Chiclayo, Chimbote, Taraboto and Chincha – and so spread its activities to the whole country. In addition, a pioneering programme in Lima itself is being considered to protect and improve the living conditions of working children in five districts of the capital. A preliminary survey was carried out between November 1991 and January 1992 in co-operation with the International Labour Office.

Through the eyes of a child

Bahay Tuluyan street children project, Malate district, Manila, Philippines

In the Philippines, the term 'street children' is generally taken to mean children who spend most of their time on the streets yet who maintain some regular contact with a family. Some 70 per cent of them go home every night and it is estimated that only about 5 per cent are completely abandoned and have no contact with families.

In 1992, the Philippines had a total population of 62 million, of whom 22 million were under the age of 15. Of these, about 70 per cent live below the poverty line and a conservative estimate, made in 1985, indicated that some 100,000 infants die annually from respiratory diseases, diarrhoea and nutritional deficiencies.

Only 2 per cent of the population has access to any type of pre-school education such as nurseries or kindergartens. For every 100 children who attend primary school, first grade, only fourteen will finish secondary school and only five will go on to complete college or vocational training courses.

The size of the problem

Some 2.4 million youngsters roam the streets of urban centres searching for some means of survival for themselves and their families. As in most Third World nations, rural-to-urban migration is taking place on a vast scale in the Philippines. Twenty-five years ago, Manila's inhabitants made up for under 5 per cent of the country's total population. Today they account for nearly 15 per cent of the total.

Traffic jams, power shortages, flooding, pollution and uncollected garbage are the most obvious indications of a general breakdown of services and an overloaded infrastructure. Less obvious are the human costs to the migrants themselves, caught up in the painful transition from a traditional way of life and an existence of survival in a city. Street children are only one manifestation of the problem, but the extent of urban poverty in the Philippines challenges the very foundations of society – it raises issues such as urban land reform, employment, a living wage, education, and so on.

Helping hands

At present, there are more than 300 agencies of all kinds working with street children in seventeen Philippine cities. Of these, 213 are non-governmental organizations and 92 are government agencies (1989 data). Over half the non-governmental organizations operate in Metropolitan Manila; 57 per cent of the agencies are community-based, 30 per cent centre-based and 12 per cent street-based.

On the face of it, these figures are impressive. Nevertheless, it has to be pointed out that, owing to limited resources, the combined services of the government agencies and the non-governmental organizations touch only about 27 per cent of the street children population. Funding problems have also meant that the

The street as a source of solidarity.

Photo: © *Hien Lam-Duc*

general social services provided by the government are often inadequate and, at times, even an obstacle to the improvement of
conditions for the young of Manila.

The struggle for survival

Children are often preferred to adults in the labour market
because they are cheaper and complain less. They are taken as
domestic help or factory and plantation workers. Altogether,
5.5 million children are estimated to be in the labour market. An
estimated 30,000 boys and girls are in the flesh trade, many of
them starting at the age of 7.

A survey conducted by the Philippine Mental Health
Association gave the following breakdown of how children
survive in the urban jungle: domestic help accounts for almost
24 per cent, as does peddling; scavenging, 19 per cent; begging,
13 per cent; car-watching, 11 per cent; prostitution, 8 per cent;
picking pockets, 4 per cent. Prostitution was found to be the
most lucrative employment, bringing in between 50 and
100 pesos a day.

The staff

The Bahay Tuluyan Centre has a permanent staff of four – three
young women and one man who serves as co-ordinator. All of
them are relatively young – in their twenties and thirties. There is
also a part-time bookkeeper. Their educational background is
varied: sociology, accounting, education and management. In
addition, a young couple with small children was invited to come

to the Centre and live there as house-father and house-mother. The house-father is a skilled carpenter and acts as a general handyman for the centre. He also serves as a useful role model for the children.

The house-mother is truly exceptional. Although not much older than the oldest of the street children, she has achieved a certain moral authority at the Centre. She, more than anyone else, is capable of taking a bottle of solvent off a child or persuading a boy to surrender his knife.

Bahay Tuluyan: a 'drop-in centre' for street children

The Bahay Tuluyan (Drop-in Centre) is situated in the Malate area, at the heart of Manila's tourist belt, where luxury hotels stand alongside smart night clubs and massage parlours.

A survey carried out in 1988, before the Bahay Tuluyan project started, revealed that there were over 3,000 street children in the area, a high percentage when compared with other districts of Metropolitan Manila.

The Malate Catholic Church has been working in the area with its Basic Christian Community (BCC) Programme for a number of years. Bahay Tuluyan, which is, in a sense, an offshoot of this programme, is a centre for alternative education which subscribes to the same principles as the BCC, namely that the community has, within itself, the resources to take care of itself; given the opportunity and a method the community can respond to its own needs; and the most effective education is when children share knowledge with their peers.

The beginning

Generally speaking, the street children in Malate have a home of some kind – usually in poor areas such as Dakota, Maria Orosa and Leveriza. However, hundreds of families also live in pushcarts parked along sidewalks or on vacant lots.

Usually the children have a relative with whom they maintain contact. This may be a mother, a father, an older sibling, an uncle, an aunt, or even a more distant relative. In many cases the contact is a neighbour, a friend or just an acquaintance.

The first stage of Bahay Tuluyan involved door-to-door visits in the poor areas near the prospective centre. A number of relatives expressed concern about the future of their children, but said they felt helpless to do anything about it.

The visits began in June 1988. At the same time, work began on the renovation of the ground floor of the Parish Centre building. A grant from the Australian Embassy paid for the construction costs and within four months the Centre was completed. The Australian Embassy grant also covered the purchase of some basic furniture such as tables and chairs.

Bahay Tuluyan came into operation on a regular basis in September 1988. Within a very short time, the staff of Bahay Tuluyan found themselves facing and responding to both long- and short-term needs, problems and objectives.

The children

The children at Bahay Tuluyan range in age from 12 months to 17 years. Most fall within the 10-to-15 age bracket. About 52 per cent are girls and 48 per cent boys. This proportion is not indicative of actual numbers on the streets, where boys far out number girls.

Children come from all over the Philippines, including the Visayan Islands and Mindanao, but almost all of them speak the national language, Tagalog.

Recently, however, there has been a large influx of refugees from Mindanao who are Badjaos. Many of these refugees live in the open by the Manila Bay sea wall, quite near the centre. Few Badjaos speak Tagalog and Bahay Tuluyan has been fortunate to recruit a young Badjao who also speaks Tagalog to be a street educator among the Badjaos.

Bahay Tuluyan is now in contact with some 300 street children, a mere handful of the estimated 3,000 in the immediate vicinity. Among these children, fifteen are Junior Educators, twenty-five belong to the Theatre Arts or Drama Groups, twenty are on the Participatory Research Team, forty to fifty are in the Day Care or Pre-school Groups and sixty regularly attend classes given by the Junior Educators. The remainder are children who come and go, who participate in the sports or other Bahay Tuluyan programmes but who do not as yet come to the Centre on a regular basis.

Child abuse

Children's motives for coming to Bahay Tuluyan are mixed, but abuse in various forms by parents or relatives is clearly a major factor in a significant number of cases. It is one of the prime reasons why some children have decided to break away from their parents permanently. Many children mention drinking and drug-taking by their parents as factors contributing to their abuse. Others put the problem down to economic difficulties and to an inability of both parents and children to raise money to maintain the family unit.

Economic difficulties are also a major reason why many children drop out of school since they are obliged to seek some kind of work to contribute to the family income. Children told stories of being ridiculed by their peers for their shabby clothing or of having to beg food from their classmates.

Not least of the benefits of the Bahay Tuluyan programme is that, generally speaking, the participants are all facing similar problems and peer pressure is reduced to a minimum.

Children teaching children:
the Junior Educators Programme

Bahay Tuluyan is basically a centre for alternative education. It acts on the principle that education is most effectively taught when children share knowledge with their peers.

Faced with a high percentage of out-of-school children and sensing that the state school system, in its present form, does not appear to meet the needs of the urban poor in general and of street children in particular, Bahay Tuluyan began its children-teaching-children experiment, the 'Junior Educators Programme', in April 1989. Young men and women – the older and regular participants, the articulate and responsible – were asked if they would be willing to join in the Centre's Education Development Programme.

The programme showed such promise in its initial stages that the Centre applied to CEBEMO (a Netherlands funding agency) for a three-year grant to develop it further. At the end of 1989, ten Junior Educators were functioning as expected within the

Bahay Tuluyan programme. These ten were selected from a total of thirty street children who were regular participants in the activities. The youngest was 11 and the oldest 17. Only one was male; two were Muslim migrants from Mindanao.

Most of them came from the poor families living in the marginalized communities around the parish church.

Objectives of the programme

The Junior Educators Programme aims to provide street children with the fundamentals they need to function effectively in society. It should enable them to understand their role in the community and be aware of their rights.

The programme employs non-conventional methods of teaching, such as drama, song and art, while striving to give a sense of care and love.

The Junior Educators have come to be regarded as junior staff of Bahay Tuluyan – in fact, one Junior Educator has become a regular staff member. It is hoped that eventually (within five to ten years) Junior Educators will be able to handle the training programmes of Bahay Tuluyan more or less on their own. The future of Bahay Tuluyan therefore lies with the Junior Educators and their training is of vital importance and taken very seriously.

The training programme

A carefully designed training programme for Junior Educators includes the following:

Syllabus-making. The Junior Educators and the regular staff, working together, select and discuss a general theme for the year and a syllabus is drawn up outlining the plan for the entire year. Each type of class, whether street-based, community-based or Centre-based, also has its own specific syllabus.

Lesson planning. The Junior Educators are taught how to prepare a plan for each lesson. The lessons are contextualized, that is, they are adapted to correspond to the situation of the street children and their environment. Every week the exact content of the lessons has to be prepared on the basis of the specific experience or circumstances touching the groups.

Teaching skills. Teaching methods include creative forms of learning such as drama, collage-making, poster-making, discussion techniques, etc. The Junior Educators attend seminars on teaching skills run by Bahay Tuluyan and attend seminars held by other agencies.

Facilitating skills. These include methods of communication which can be used both in the classroom and in community meetings. They are taught how to encourage participation on the part of students and how to involve parents.

Human relations training. Instruction in how to relate more effectively to both other children and adults.

Reporting. This includes training in documenting and evaluating classwork content, procedures and results. An element of self-evaluation is included.

Complementary training activities for Junior Educators

Junior Educators also attend other seminars and training sessions, including:

Self-discovery sessions. These are designed to promote self-understanding and the recognition of potential and weaknesses.

Value formation seminars. The purpose of these seminars is to help Junior Educators set priorities for themselves in their lives.

Leadership seminars. These are designed to help Junior Educators become effective leaders.

Retreats. These offer an opportunity for the Junior Educators to reflect, pray and reinforce their motivation.

Symposia. These cover a variety of topics such as the national situation, agrarian reform, the Church, etc. They are sponsored by other organizations, and the Junior Educators and other children of the Centre are encouraged to attend.

The present group of Junior Educators is the second group to have been trained for this important role. Many former Junior Educators have now joined the Centre's Peer Counselling Programme.

Non-formal education

The non-formal education dispensed at Bahay Tuluyan differs from the formal education of the regular schools in a number of ways:

- No payment is solicited.
- Participants are not asked to buy items needed for projects (a common practice in formal education).
- There is very little in the way of structure, such as seating plans, uniforms, etc.
- Students are regularly asked to evaluate the method, their instructors and their classmates.
- The method builds on the considerable experience that students already have (for example, when it comes to

mathematics, many have worked or are working in selling or supplying goods or services and already know a lot of practical mathematics).

- Course duration is not strictly fixed but depends upon the students' skills, knowledge and interest.
- Students are encouraged to develop at their own pace.
- Drop-outs are almost non-existent, partly due to a sense of belonging and partly to the fact that students participate in designing and carrying out the course.
- Grades are not given. Co-operation rather than competition is encouraged. Students are made to understand that each one of them is unique and has special abilities.

Bahay Tuluyan sees itself primarily as a centre for alternative education, either supplying education to those who do not attend formal school or supplementing it for those who do. However, since diplomas and certificates are all-important in obtaining employment, the Bahay Tuluyan staff (with some misgivings) encourage children to enter formal education.

Participants in the programmes can qualify for scholarships for formal education. Scholarships are available for elementary and secondary school. Two scholarship children are already in college and are regarded by the Centre as potential future staff members.

Street-based and community-based programmes

It takes a great deal of creativity to run an educational pro-gramme on a street corner. However, most children, whatever their situation in life, are interested in education and, if the methodology is participative, most will respond.

Most of the children find formal education boring and

time-consuming, yet in Filipino society, elementary and high-school diplomas are held in high esteem. On the other hand, the children find informal education, conducted through dialogue, comparatively interesting, but the programme is not recognized by the Department of Education and Culture and is therefore less useful to parents and students when it comes to applying for a job. It is also quite difficult to sustain interest for long periods on a street corner where a significant number of the students also work and have many acquaintances.

The community-based education programme – where a vacant space or a chapel in a poor urban area can be used for teaching sessions – holds more promise.

Day care or pre-school classes

Some of the Junior Educators run morning classes for one group and afternoon classes for another. Most of the children in these groups are of pre-school age and live in poor urban areas near Bahay Tuluyan or in push-carts parked near the centre.

Many of the children are preparing for formal schooling in the coming school year. Their parents work as waiters or laundrywomen or are, in some way, involved in the tourist trade in the area. For some it is the only school they will ever attend.

Emphasis is on co-operation rather than competition and at the formal graduation ceremony every year everyone receives some kind of award (the cleanest child, the most punctual, etc.) so as to develop self-esteem at an early age. To some extent, the day-care programme is a preventive measure designed to keep the children off the streets.

The Theatre Arts Group

The children's experiences provide most of the themes for the street theatre. Members of the group are challenged – according to their inclinations – to compose songs, write poems, take photographs or produce plays or dances about situations that have been discussed by the group.

Such a situation might, for instance, be that of a child who has been severely beaten by a relative and has been asked to express the experience through an art form. Two years ago, a group of parents, children and supporters marched on the Commission for Immigration to demand the deportation of a foreign paedophile guilty of abusing a number of children.

The group put on a drama in the plaza outside the Commission portraying the reason for the march. It was a far more effective means of communication with the spectators than any number of speeches could have been.

Vocational training

Tagalog, of the variety commonly spoken in Manila rather than the purer form spoken in the surrounding provinces, is the medium of communication for all the vocational training classes at the centre.

Electricity. Eighteen of the older youths attend classes in electricity at the centre. The instructor is a former Junior Educator who showed an aptitude for electrical work. Bahay Tuluyan helped him to receive formal training to become a professional electrician and now he has become the instructor for the classes at the Centre. Using the training he received as a Junior Educator, he employs the non-formal methods of discussion and 'hands-on' techniques.

Typing. Nearly all participants at Bahay Tuluyan have been in a typing class at one time or another. As only a limited number of typewriters are available, students practise with a piece of paper with a drawn keyboard. They then take it in turns to practise on the few real typewriters. The Junior Educators and members of the participatory research team usually type out their reports and even the staff reports are typed out by members of the class.

Sewing. Sewing classes are run by the Bahay Tuluyan house-mother. She teaches a dozen or so students who can now make school uniforms and clothes for themselves and for others. Last year, the children of Bahay Tuluyan were invited to take part in a ceremony for the elderly. They presented a traditional Filipino dance and the dancers' costumes were all designed and produced by members of the sewing class.

Music. Although classified here as 'vocational', the music classes are, in fact, essential to the overall educational method used by Bahay Tuluyan. Music plays an important role in Philippine culture and is recognized as being an extremely powerful medium of expression. Children can learn to play the flute and/or the guitar and they are encouraged to write their own songs and to teach others to do the same. Christmas parties include pieces by the 'Flute Ensemble'. The flutes they play are not of the type used in professional orchestras but a plastic variety that is readily available in the Philippines. The country is also a net exporter of guitars, so a relatively good guitar can be obtained at a reasonable price.

Peer counselling:
street children are their own best confidants

Drugs (mainly solvent-sniffing) and the violence arising from drugs are a common problem among street children and the cause of many of their emotional troubles. In attempting to respond to this problem, Bahay Tuluyan tends to turn to the street children themselves rather than to someone with academic qualifications, on the basis that children might prove to be more effective than adults as counsellors for other children.

This was the thinking behind the recent Peer Counselling Programme, launched with the aid of a grant from Save the Children Fund in the United Kingdom. The major difficulty in launching the group was finding someone capable of translating their theoretical knowledge into terms for children, someone capable of convincing the children that counselling is a normal human activity in which everyone is constantly engaged and that, with some refinement and the growth of confidence, most people can become good at it.

Former Junior Educators have been invited to become peer counsellors and a psychologist has been running two Saturday sessions a month for a group of fifteen participants. So far, the psychologist has been teaching group dynamics and common counselling techniques. As the programme progresses and the counsellors take over the programme, it is hoped that they will be able to hold sessions for other children.

The Participatory Research Team

Like counselling, research is a normal human activity. Children learn a lot from listening to one another. If their experiences could be structured and they could be encouraged to observe, listen and talk to one another, their research into the problems of street children could well prove to be more valuable than that undertaken by professional researchers.

Discussions within this group are always lively and nearly always seem to demand additional research. Research by street children into the problems of street children (why children go into prostitution; why they sniff solvents) would definitely be worth publishing. These exercises have been rich and very helpful in terms of self-discovery and understanding.

Embryo projects

The staff of Bahay Tuluyan are full of ideas for expanding their work alongside the street children of Manila. Two such schemes are still in an embryo stage.

The paramedical programme

A tentative start has been made with this scheme which has proved to have potential but requires time, more funding and talented leadership to succeed. Inspired by the Junior Educators scheme, the plan is to have Junior Paramedics in the community.

In one dramatic case, children in the programme were responsible for saving a child's life. The child's parents had failed to recognize the symptoms of meningitis, but when the children went to visit their sick friend they realized straight away that he was seriously ill. They alerted the Bahay Tuluyan staff and he was rushed to hospital.

Uncontrolled urban growth creates slums.
These children do not have running water in the house
and must collect it from taps in the street.
Photo: © UNICEF/Francene Keery

A night shelter

For some time now, Bahay Tuluyan has been looking for a site for a night shelter where children who have no other place to stay for the night could go and receive an evening meal and breakfast before going back on to the streets. Such a shelter would both help meet some children's short-term needs and serve as an initiation to the Bahay Tuluyan programme. New children coming into the programme need a period of orientation so as to be able to 'catch up' with the rest of the group.

Unfortunately, land prices are very high in the inner city area and at present the night shelter remains no more than a plan.

Funding

In the words of Bahay Tuluyan itself, 'finances have been, at best, a hit or miss affair'. Contributions have been received from a number of sources:

- CEBEMO has given a three-year grant for the Junior Educators Programme (now in its third year).
- Save the Children Fund (UK) has given grants for the Peer Counselling Programme and for emergency needs.
- The Australian Embassy has been generous, not only in the construction of the Centre, but also with regard to equipment for the sewing and typing classes.
- Terre des Hommes has helped fund the Health Programme.
- Visitors to the Centre – including students, representatives from various religious groups, a group of Japanese expatriates, a group from Germany, supporters from Hawaii and friends from New York – have also been very generous.

- In the Philippines, private individuals and small businesses have given what they could.

Finances need to be put on a firmer basis to enable the group to plan ahead. To be able to experiment with programmes, the staff need to know that the budget is assured, at least for one year.

An island in a sea of want

The Bahay Tuluyan project has been described as 'a humble enterprise in a sea of want'. It is indeed a humbling thought that, of an estimated 3,000 street children in the immediate vicinity, Bahay Tuluyan is in regular contact with 200 and irregular contact with a further 100.

The education dispensed at Bahay Tuluyan may, at times, cause conflict. Among other things, children are taught that they have certain rights. Once they have overcome their initial disbelief, the children become more articulate and assertive. Not everyone likes children (and this includes some parents) when they become articulate and assertive.

When they begin to test the water and exercise their rights, conflict sometimes ensues. (A Manila policeman rarely wants to listen to vagrant children declaiming about their supposed rights.)

But if Bahay Tuluyan is a 'humble enterprise', humility is the key to its success. There is a very genuine effort to come to grips with the problems of street children by attempting to see the world through the eyes of the children themselves.

The Junior Educators Programme, the Peer Counselling Progamme and the Participatory Research Team – all of which are based on this principle – are experiments which have proved their worth.

A number of children from Bahay Tuluyan have been reunited with their families; some have put drugs behind them; others have served time in gaol. Representatives from each of these categories are now assisting in the Centre's alternative forms of education and helping other children like themselves.

The finances of Bahay Tuluyan need a firmer foundation. It has, however, a key message to give to other agencies. The message is simple enough yet difficult to implement – to help street children we must look at their problems through the eyes of a child.

Reinsertion through work

Street or working children have, in many cases, dropped out of school or never been to school at all. Forced to work to support their families or beg for themselves, they have never had the time or money to think in terms of education. Moreover, organized and formal schooling is all the more alien to children used to the chaos of the street. Education appears as yet another laborious process without concrete results or immediate gain.

Rehabilitation and education, however, can take on different forms, and work, as opposed to the notion of schooling in the traditional sense, can be just as effective in introducing the child to society and its rules. Work and training have the advantage of producing immediate results and satisfaction, not to mention the possibility of a small but psychologically significant income.

Work experiences and the very concept of work vary from country to country but a fundamental ideal remains: the child or adolescent is producing and, by producing, is developing into an active member of society. The Atelier Bon Conseil in Togo provides a good example of rehabilitation through work. The founders have showed how exploitation must stop and partnership, with the children, begin. The students not only learn as they produce but also earn. This means the child is given a vital boost of confidence and self-esteem. Children begin to realize the capacity that lies within them. In the Don Bosco project in Medellín, Colombia, work is considered essential in the moulding of new personalities; the children understand that they alone are responsible for earning and that they can live without resorting to criminal activities. Productivity and income appear as answers and as the major rules that regulate society.

Work and training, as in the Boys' Society of Sierra Leone, are completely devoid of any notion of paternalism and charity. The educators know that the children deserve the income they receive and that they have become part of the production cycle.

The street boys of Freetown

Street children project, The Boys' Society of Sierra Leone, Freetown, Sierra Leone

Freetown stands at the crossroads of the social, political and economic life of Sierra Leone. It is a city of contrasts where elegant buildings overlook shacks and the highly visible élite constitutes an ever-present reminder of economic and social disparities.

It has been estimated that more than 40 per cent of the population of Freetown is under the age of 15 and that tens of thousands of deprived, homeless children eke out a precarious existence on the streets.

The Boys' Society of Sierra Leone

In 1966, a group of Sierra Leoneans and expatriate residents of Freetown founded the Boys' Society of Sierra Leone to assist in the rehabilitation of underprivileged, homeless and often delinquent boys. Freetown is a multi-religious community and the decision to cater for boys only was taken to avoid offending religious susceptibilities concerning the mixing of the sexes and the training of young women for jobs traditionally reserved for men.

This decision was taken for purely local reasons and clearly cannot, in any way, be considered to be of universal application.

For several years, the Society's activities focused on community service projects and sport. The boys of the Society became responsible for the landscaping, beautifying and maintenance of historic sites, commercial zones and tourist areas within the city. The sporting programme deliberately fostered a spirit of healthy competition and sportsmanship among the children who had little other opportunity to direct their physical energy in positive directions.

The current programme organization

The overall programme is headed by a Programme Director who receives guidance from an Advisory Board consisting of professionals from varying disciplines. The Programme Director is the Chief Executive and heads the General Administration Sector. He is assisted by a Deputy Programme Director, a confidential secretary and a typist.

There are, at present, three programme sectors: Welfare and Publicity (consisting of one Co-ordinator, one Assistant Co-ordinator and three trained Social Workers); Education and Training (one Co-ordinator and one trained Social Worker); Income Generation (a Workshop Manager, supervised by the Deputy Programme Director). There used to be Residential and Health Care programmes, but these were phased out early in 1990 as financial resources were lacking.

A zoning system

When it became clear that the need for such activities was city-wide, the programme was made more manageable by dividing the city into several zones. Each zone had a recognized Zone Leader backed by assistants. Then, for each zone a maximum of fifty members was selected on the basis of real need.

The zones, thereafter, become part of the Society's Welfare and Publicity Sector, which is responsible for recruiting boys to the programme through its outreach activities.

At present 648 severely disadvantaged boys have been registered. They come from sixteen neighbourhoods or zones. The members themselves elect Zone Leaders and assistants annually under the supervision of Social Workers and Publicity Co-ordinators.

For administrative purposes the boys are divided into three categories – those attending school, those enrolled in skills training classes and those not in school and not enrolled in training classes. This third group forms the pool from which boys are selected for enrolment in skills-training programmes. All other activities, such as inter-zonal sports and athletics competitions, and weekend community service projects, are organized by the Zone Leaders with the help of the Social Workers.

Parent Action Committees are organized in each zone and they are used by the Social Workers and Welfare Co-ordinators as catalysts for counselling the boys, identifying training areas, planning community projects and so on.

Parents also receive counselling from welfare officials to help them to understand that they too must assume responsibility for the care of their children.

Objectives

- To provide behavioural guidance to boys aged 8 to 18.
- To promote the health, social, educational, vocational and character development of young, underprivileged boys.

- To facilitate valid out-of-school activities through the development of zonal action.
- To provide support for underprivileged and neglected street boys with their rehabilitation as the ultimate goal.

Learning to be

The process of selecting boys for school support or for vocational training begins with intensive fieldwork by the Co-ordinators and Social Workers.

Meetings are held in each zone to identify those, already enrolled with the Society, who might need enrolling in training schemes or educational support. Lists of possible candidates are prepared and submitted to the Education and Training Co-ordinator, who undertakes the various enrolments.

Other boys, who are not members of the Society, may be put forward by parents and, following intensive interviewing by the Education and Training Co-ordinator or the Welfare Co-ordinator, they may be selected for a place.

When these recruitment drives take place, boys who show interest are registered within the appropriate zone. Those who appear to be academically strong are encouraged to enter the formal school system; those who are academically weaker are encouraged to opt for vocational training.

Formal schooling

The Society currently supports 530 boys enrolled in Freetown's primary and secondary schools. Each year, the Education Co-ordinator identifies the individual needs of these students (school fees, school uniform, exercise books, etc.) and authorizes pay-

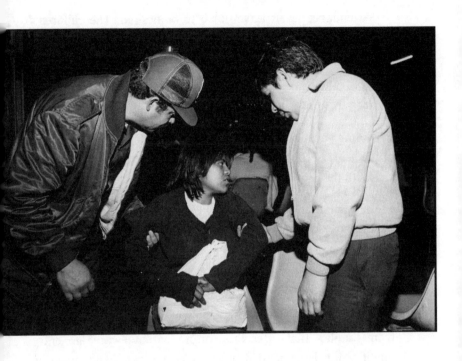

Young prostitute sleeping in a station.
In some countries, boys are involved as much as girls,
and are often no older than 9.
Photo: © UNICEF/Francene Keery

ment. Continuation of this educational support is conditional on satisfactory academic performance and participation in the Society's community service projects.

Attendance levels leave much to be desired. The children's economic and social background is such that motivation at the family level is very low, resulting frequently in dropping out.

Learn to earn

Providing vocational training for underprivileged street boys lies at the heart of the Society's activities.

With the help of highly qualified technicians and trainers, the Boys' Society has drawn up curricula in metalwork, car-body work, car mechanics, car electrics, lathe operation, carpentry, agriculture and tailoring.

Entry qualifications

Since the boys selected for training are underprivileged and come from families that offer little or no parental care, no entry qualification is demanded other than age (candidates must be between the ages of 14 and 22) and an evident readiness to learn a trade.

Boys recruited directly through the identification and recruitment programme and those not quite 14 years old are sent to the Regent Agricultural Centre where they are prepared to join other training establishments.

Boys from the zones recommended for training opportunities by the Welfare Department are sent directly to the Society's Production and Training Centre or to the Carpentry Unit. If there are insufficient places for all of them in the Society's own centres, places are found in outside training establishments. Regular visits are made to these establishments to monitor the trainees' attendance, general progress and performance, and to give them counselling. The nature and quality of the training given is also under permanent review.

The normal training period is three years. One month before the completion of training, boys are transferred to the Production and Training Centre or the Carpentry Unit for observation and assessment. They then take the Trade Tests conducted by the programme and, if successful, are awarded the Boys' Society of Sierra Leone Test Certificate.

The Agricultural Centre

In 1976, the Society leased 6 hectares of land at Regent Village, some 12 kilometres from the centre of Freetown. The land was gradually developed into nurseries for seedlings, potted plants and Christmas trees, vegetable gardens, a medium-sized rice paddy, a small plantation of fuel-wood trees and a small animal husbandry unit, all of which are geared towards generating funds for the Society.

Trainees at the Agricultural Centre are boarders and are provided with food, shelter and basic health care. Emotional security, protection against harassment, character development and counselling are provided by the resident staff and the Education Co-ordinator. All trainees receive a small monthly allowance. The skills centre is self-financing. Jobs are accepted on a commercial basis and profits are put back in to increase outside funding.

The Society owns a workshop in Freetown which serves as a

main skills-training centre. The centre has about forty-five trainees at any one time; other candidates for skills training are placed at privately owned workshops within the city.

The skills-training scheme, which started in 1986, concentrates on highly marketable skills such as car mechanics, metalwork, bodywork, refrigerator repairs, carpentry and tailoring. Recently, block-laying and the manufacture of roofing tiles have been added. The training period varies according to the skill, but it generally ranges from two to four years. The workshop is headed by a Workshop Manager with overall supervision by the Deputy Programme Director.

The Society's principal income-generating component, the Workshop, has been self-financing since 1986, when Caritas (Germany) bought the premises of a once well-known garage to serve as the Society's vocational training centre. Since January 1988 10 per cent of its net monthly income has been placed in a fund which is passed on to the Society for use in other sectors.

There is a work force of twenty-six technicians who provide the trainees with practical on-the-job tuition, and this practical instruction is backed up by theoretical sessions so the boys understand the basic underlying principles of their fields of training.

About a year ago, a new beginners' carpentry programme was established at the Society's headquarters building in John Street. This was a step forward in plans to expand the Society's training facilities. This workshop is staffed by one technical instructor, and the objectives are to captivate the boys' interest and prepare them for transfer to the main carpentry section.

Training at the main Carpentry Unit lasts four years. The best trainees, however, sometimes complete the course in three years and are then allowed to apply to become quasi-employees, receiving incentive payments related to the productivity of the Carpentry Unit. Boys placed in outside workshops usually work six days a week. Outside workshops are monitored to ensure that the trainees are not exploited or overworked.

Dropping out

Regular attendance is one of the main problems facing the Society. The drop-out rate in the vocational sector is about 20 per cent and this is mainly due to the fact that expectations of making quick money are not fulfilled. Moreover, some trainees change their minds as they grow older. A small number have had to be expelled following serious cases of theft.

The major handicap, however, is the boys' social, economic and family background. Many of them come from families in very poor economic condition, from broken homes, one-parent homes or polygamous homes. Most of the boys are, therefore, in difficult or disadvantageous situations and show signs of not having had proper family care.

The Society tries to increase motivation by establishing a tripartite relationship involving the family, the boy and the programme. The family is taught the importance of vocational training so that, at least, the boy will receive its moral support. The training staff are also educated to understand the problems of the boys the Society caters for.

Teachers, instructors and trainers

Apart from one full-time qualified tutor, who provides remedial education for some of the boys enrolled in vocational training schemes, the Society is not a direct employer of teachers from formal education.

The Society's vocational training staff are all male, aged 25 to 55. The chief instructors are all professionally qualified, but about 90 per cent of the vocational trainers in the private workshops and training centres have no professional qualifications. They have all been through the apprenticeship system, however, and are proficient in their various skills. The trainers in the workshops are full-time, salaried employees; those working in outside workshops are self-employed and receive no payment from the Society.

Planning for success

Vocational training is the keystone of the Boys' Society of Sierra Leone's activities and careful planning is the reason for its success.

The Society's workshops – which are not only self-supporting but also capable of generating a surplus income towards running costs – form the backbone of, and a model for, the programme. However, since these workshops can only cater for about forty-five trainees at a time, innovative ways have been found to provide places for many more children. This is done by making use of existing, recognized vocational training institutions as well as privately owned workshops. To be included in the scheme any position offered by a private workshop must clearly be a training activity and not merely a job.

One of the more surprising yet most logical innovations is that rather than demand that the boys be qualified to learn, the Society insists that the training institutions be qualified to teach this type of boy. The only qualifications demanded of any child wanting to enter the training scheme are that he genuinely wants to learn a trade, is a registered member of the Society and is aged between 14 and 22.

The role of the Training and Education Co-ordinator is crucial to the successful implementation of the training scheme. He forms the link between the Society, the trainees and the trainers. He is a powerful motivating force behind the trainee. His role is to impress upon the trainee the dignity of the trade he is embarking on, to guide him through the difficult moments that will occur as he encounters new experiences, to be an advocate for the trainee in his relationship with the trainer and to go through assessment reports with the trainee so that he will be fully aware of the strengths and weaknesses his trainer has observed.

As regards the trainer, the Co-ordinator's first task is to convince him of the benefits he will gain by taking on the Society's trainees. Once a trainee has been accepted, the Co-ordinator meets the trainer regularly to discuss the work required, the training given and any progress. He will also negotiate with the trainer on the trainee's behalf for improved conditions as the latter's contribution increases.

At the end of the initial six months of the work, an assessment is made of the minimum/maximum length for total training. It is important for the trainee to know when he will, at least to some extent, be completely 'trained'.

All the trainees in the vocational training scheme receive a small monthly allowance from the Society. In addition, most trainers in the non-Society workshops tip trainees whenever they have well-paid jobs in their workshops.

A savings scheme for trainees

A plan of enforced saving is an integral part of the training scheme. The objective is to reinforce the idea that saving is an important aspect of being employed. Furthermore, it provides a lump sum for the boy when he completes his training assignment and can contribute to the cost of job-related tools.

Employment after training

Although the Society recognizes that there is a need to help with job placement after training, this has as yet not been undertaken. Small grants are, however, available to encourage some of the boys to become self-employed. The plan for the future is to encourage ex-trainees with similar or complementary skills to form small groups and practise their skills commercially. This however would require additional funding which is currently not available.

The overall scope of the Society's activities is restricted by the level of funding. The major funding partner has always stressed the need for self-sufficiency, but self-sufficiency requires a substantial cash flow. There is also a need for a staff training and development scheme to ensure the continued growth of the programme.

Funding

Founded in 1966 by a group of Sierra Leoneans and expatriate residents of Freetown, the Boys' Society of Sierra Leone is a local foundation whose activities have attracted support from a wide variety of agencies (including Terre des Hommes (the Netherlands), the Catholic Relief Services, the United Christian Council, the Canadian Universities Services Overseas and the British High Commission) as well as from private individuals from within the country. In 1984, Caritas (Germany), in partnership with the German Government, agreed to fund various aspects of the entire programme. Since then, Caritas has been the programme's major funding agency.

Funds are geared to three-year phases of the programme. The third of these phases ended in 1993. Although grants will continue to be needed for the Society to press ahead with its development plans, every effort is being made to ensure that, in the long term, the Society will achieve its goal of becoming entirely self-supporting.

The Boys' Society of Sierra Leone is a remarkable organization in many ways:

- As its name implies, it is for boys only.
- Unlike many other organizations for helping street children it was founded and is run by local people – the residents of Freetown.
- Although it supports street boys who want to go to school, it is not in competition with the local school system. Apart from a small remedial education unit to assist those boys in its vocational training scheme who ask for help, it employs no teachers in the field of formal school teaching.
- It demands no qualifications from those who seek to use its services other than membership of the Society and a desire to help themselves.
- It provides basic health care, one meal each workday for its vocational trainees, access to sporting activities and libraries, career counselling, and moral support and motivation.

- It accepts gifts from charitable organizations but is working hard to become self-supporting.

It does not offer charity, but a fighting chance to escape from the despair and poverty of the streets.

Civic responsibility

The non-training aspects of the Society's activities – the community service and sporting activities carried out in the zones into which Freetown is divided – are intended to inculcate a sense of fair play and civic responsibility, qualities that are often sadly absent in youngsters who lack any parental guidance or control.

Through their work in beautifying and maintaining the grounds of historic sites, commercial and tourist areas, the boys learn to take a pride in the appearance of their zones. This is enhanced by the fact that the boys elect their own Zone Leaders who, with the help of trained social workers, are responsible for the smooth running of zonal activities.

Whilst the notions of community service and the provision of access to sporting facilities are highly commendable, they are common to very many initiatives around the world. For the Boys' Society of Sierra Leone they are important also as being the initial point of contact with the street boys.

Three key factors

There are three key, interlinked factors in the Society's approach to vocational training which could well be copied in other schemes.

The scheme has been devised from a street boy's point of view.
Since the only qualifications for entry, apart from age (14
to 22), are membership of the Society and a demonstrated
desire to learn, the door of opportunity is open to all, even
the hardened school drop-out or the boy who has never been
to school. Training is on-the-job and, unlike school lessons,
clearly applicable to the street boy's immediate concerns,
that is, food and training now, a possible career later. The
boys receive a small allowance but they do not feel that this is
charity since they know that what they do brings a small
return to the Society.

The Society's determination to make the scheme self-supporting.
The link with the previous point is obvious. If the scheme can
be made fully self-supporting, any suspicion of charity
disappears. The boys will really feel that they are doing their
own thing.

*Persuading outside workshop owners of the benefits of taking on
trainees.* By linking outside workshop owners with the
scheme and persuading them to follow the Society's training
curricula, the places available for trainees can be multiplied
exponentially. It also leads to the establishment of the
Society's curricula as the accepted local norm.

The ABC of training

Atelier Bon Conseil, Togo

Togo is the 'thin man' of West Africa. Situated on the Gulf of Guinea, it is bordered to the east by Benin and to the west by Ghana and has a total surface area of 54,000 km². From the Atlantic in the south to Burkina Faso in the north, it stretches some 600 km but at its widest, from east to west, it measures 150 km and its coastline a mere 50 km. The 1981 census put the population of Togo at 2.72 million. Today it is estimated to be 3.5 million, of whom half are under the age of 15. Some 75 per cent of the population live in rural areas, but over the last two decades the urban population growth rate has accelerated and remains twice that of the rural areas. Apart from the mining and commercialization of phosphates, the country's economy is based mainly on the export of agricultural produce, such as cocoa, coffee, cotton and oleaginous products.

The old made new

In Togo, as in most African countries south of the Sahara, almost all manufactured goods, even the most simple, are imported. Manpower is certainly not lacking, but there is a shortage of skilled craftsmen and technicians capable of carrying out repairs competently or of making good quality articles. The number of motor mechanics, for example, would appear to be greater than the total number of vehicles in the country. If your vehicle breaks down in the middle of Lomé, you are likely to find yourself surrounded by a group of young people offering to carry out the necessary repairs at a price and a speed defying all competition.

Like the shoeshine boys, these young 'street mechanics' roam the streets of the city from dawn till dusk, a bag of tools on their shoulders, in search of stranded motorists. Most of these mechanics are, however, no more than inefficient handymen who have been badly trained in local workshops and who, more often than not, even succeed in damaging brand-new spare parts. And this is true in all fields that require very precise qualifications.

Moreover, most of these handymen are young people who have dropped out of school with no qualifications and are unable to earn a decent living from their work. And unfortunately they represent only a minority among tens of thousands of others in the same situation, with no future and not even the chance of becoming even inefficient handymen. What is more, no viable alternative is open to them. Their almost total exclusion from national development programmes takes on the appearance of normal and deserved punishment for having committed the 'error' of not succeeding at school. Nevertheless, the government recognizes the need to train craftsmen for the informal, modern sector. It also recognizes that 'entrepreneurs responsible for training do not always have the required technical and pedagogical competence'.[1] The fear is that the administrative

---

1. *Cadre macro-économique 1991–1995.* Document prepared in 1990 for the Second Conference of Funding Agencies for the Development of Togo.

Education is the only way to bring street children back
into society and help them to build a future for themselves.
Photo: *Dominic Sansoni*

solution envisaged (a restructuring of the apprenticeship system) will do nothing to change the situation since it is based on the existing system. New training structures for technicians and apprenticeships need to be introduced, not only for the sake of the national economy but also, and primarily, for the benefit of human development.

Since everything is imported and little is repaired, there are many materials in Togo that could be recovered and recycled. In industrialized countries, particularly, there are tools, both new and second-hand, from the simplest to the most sophisticated, which have been rendered obsolete by scientific advance or commercial competition. These outdated tools are often set aside as waste or scrap. Yet many of them could be overhauled and given a new lease of life in Togo. In the same way, tailings and off-cuts of metals and plastics of all sorts, regarded as waste in industrialized countries, could be re-used in Togo.

Training the deprived young

Considerations such as these led Urs Bischofberger, a young Swiss mechanic and voluntary aid worker, and his Togolese partner Léon Djimeto Djossou to found the Centre de Formation Professionnelle 'Atelier Bon Conseil' (ABC) at Agome-Kpalime, Kloto region, in 1980.

For some, this name might evoke the *Bon Pasteur* (the Good Stepherd), as though the founders hoped to 'rescue' young people, lost in the modern jungle of hazards and guide them towards better living conditions.

To a certain extent this could be considered a correct interpretation since, when it was created, the Centre was called 'Atelier Bon

Conseil – Soyez Exigeants!' And indeed, backed by the professio-
nalism and experience of their instructors, those who are trained at
the Centre are expected to demand much of themselves and to
encourage their customers to do the same. This suggests that the
instructors and the apprentices hold the quality of their products
and services in high esteem and this in a country that is not yet
industrialized. Above all, this stems from the fact that this is a private initiative based on a will to contribute to the country's development. It aims to train deprived young people, without any sense
of ethnocentric paternalism or complacency.

The ABC is inscribed on the Togo register of commerce as 'a
company specialized, mainly in Africa and more particularly in
the Republic of Togo, in the provision of professional training in
all trades'. It is conceived of as being an alternative or a
complement to state or state-supported programmes. It shares
the same objectives but avoids the government's bureaucracy
and lack of concern for financial autonomy – obstacles that often
appear to stand in the way of the country's true development.
There are a few companies and professional training centres that
place similar emphasis on quality, but their training is very
expensive.

From the beginning, the Atelier Bon Conseil has sought to
provide a direct service to its target group of young school
drop-outs in difficulty and to the public at large which supplies
its commercial customers. The town of Kpalime was selected as
headquarters. It is the capital of the Kloto region, one of the
most populous regions of the country with a population growth
rate to match Lomé's. The choice was a judicious one since, in
this extremely agricultural region known for its food and cash
crops, the need for tools, craftsmen and their services is high.

Furthermore, by encouraging young artisans to set up in the

region, the Centre is helping to stem the tide of young people leaving rural areas while, at the same time, enhancing the, prestige of the crafts and technical trades. Such trades, in comparison with jobs obtainable after formal schooling, have traditionally been seen as the last resort.

Finally, the Centre guards against the exploitation of children and young people in workshops. There are, in fact, many artisan employers who, disregarding the traditional conditions of apprenticeship, which were formerly above reproach, exploit scores of apprentices whom they see as an easy source of money .

A miniature factory

To attain his objective, Urs Bischofberger went to considerable lengths to 'sell' his idea to a number of Swiss and German industrialists. Once this was achieved he had little difficulty in enrolling young Togolese who had been rejected not only by the ordinary schools but even by the technical schools.

The Atelier Bon Conseil covers a wide range of activities, but its purpose is twofold – the production of goods and the transmission of knowledge and know-how. In this way it hopes to meet the needs of a wide clientele consisting of individuals, artisans, industrialists, businessmen, state services, and so on. 'Let us recover everything, re-use everything and recycle anything that can be of use. Let us be imaginative. Our motto is: "The impossible we achieve immediately; miracles take a little longer." ' These words provide a perfect illustration of the spirit that underlies the Atelier Bon Conseil. The first team consisted of the two founders and a number of well-qualified temporary staff from the German-speaking areas of Switzerland. In April 1983, for example, three young Swiss, Stephan and

Christophe Sonderegger, and René Niederer, visited the Atelier Bon Conseil and decided to make their own contribution to its development over the next few years. They, in turn, ran the General Mechanics and Fitting Department, and the Joinery and Carpentry Department. The polytechnic aspect of the Centre is reflected in its structure. There are several training and production departments designed to meet the priority needs of the population: General Mechanics and Fitting; Joinery and Carpentry; Locksmith and Welding; Mechanical and Electrical Car Fitting; Bodywork and Painting; Utility Vehicles; Building; Transport and Goods Handling; Refrigeration, Electricity and Plumbing.

Hampered by a shortage of financial resources, the Centre was first established on a small piece of rented land. Then, following the positive reaction of the Swiss industrialists, the dream became a reality and, with its first earnings, the team was able to acquire another 300 m^2 of land. The present workshop was built on this site and came into service in July 1993. With a preliminary load of second-hand tools, sent from Europe without charge or bought cheaply and reconditioned on the spot, the Centre was gradually transformed over the years into a successful operational factory. The Centre continues to receive aid from international development organizations, and from political and church communities.

Despite its growth, the Centre still employs a relatively small number of staff. At present the Atelier Bon Conseil employs two Swiss volunteers, an assistant manager, an accountant, a secretary, a general supervisor, ten qualified workmen, a professional teaching supervisor and eight heads of department, giving a ratio of 25 staff to 120 apprentices.

Most of the spare parts are made from salvaged materials. Various kinds of motors are made from spare parts found on the scrap-metal market (pistons, crankshafts from cars, tractors, etc.). With the exception of complicated items such as injection pumps and the injectors themselves, everything is made in the workshop. What is more, the Centre improves, transforms and invents machines. Many projects have been devoted to the creation and manufacture of small machines for general use such as coffee pulpers, coconut splitters, solar water-heaters, wind-operated pumps and small diesel electricity generators capable of providing power for machinery in areas where electricity is not yet generally available. Creative imagination also has a part to play in the recovery and re-use of obsolete items – an old lorry chassis can very well be used to form the framework of a small bridge on a minor road, the engine of a damaged tractor can be used to run a dynamo, and so on.

All these activities require a constantly available stock of 'raw materials'. As far as possible, everything has to be stored because, sooner or later, everything can be put to good use. To hold these supplies the Centre has a full, well-ordered main storehouse with a stock-holding area of 1,500 m^2. This is highly important, pedagogically speaking, as the young apprentices need to learn to keep things in order, and to forecast and control the stock. In short, this is the basic methodology of artisanal and industrial stock control.

Over the years, the range of activities at the Centre grew, its property and the services it provided diversified and the number of customers increased. It became more and more difficult to respect delivery dates. The data provided by the accounting system were insufficient to enable the management to take clear and rapid decisions and make proper short- and long-term plans. The management system had to be modified. In November 1989, however, the Centre introduced a new and clearer accounting system so that information on any current operation could be readily unearthed. As a result of these modifications, the accounting, administration and management services have become less centralized, each department has been given greater autonomy and performance assessment has become much easier.

Made in Togo

The production departments are the key 'instruments' of training and education. The organization and functioning of these departments and above all the efficiency of apprentices' supervision are crucial to the quality of the training. This is why the most important departments where knowledge and solid practical experience are vital have been under the guidance of instructors trained in Swiss workshops. In 1983, René Niederer took over the General Mechanics and Fitting Department, three years after completing his own training at Leica (Heerbrugg, Switzerland). Similarly, Stephan Sonderegger took over the Joinery and Carpentry Department in 1986 after training at the Metallbau workshop. Urs Bischofberger was himself a mechanic and obtained professional experience in Swiss workshops and aid centres before perfecting his knowledge of almost all areas of artisanal techniques – bakery/pastry-making, catering and nutrition, electricity, water supply and plumbing, civil engineering, etc. The first Togolese instructors were recruited after technical study in Europe (Belgium and former Czechoslovakia) and were then trained by the Atelier Bon Conseil.

General Mechanics and Fitting Department

The structure, equipment and production capacity of the General Mechanics and Fitting Department make it unique in all Togo. All sorts of spare parts are made there and all manner of repairs are carried out for customers in the town, the region and country but also for the other departments. The work involves threading, sawing, filing, drilling, all kinds of fitting, the manufacture and repair of numerous parts for the Mechanical and Electrical Car Fitting Department, etc.

At present, this department employs a department head, an instructor and two workmen, and thirteen apprentices. It also welcomes three or four visiting probationers each year to come and 'explore the realities' of working in Third World conditions. Since this department became operational, the space allocated to it has been doubled (from 100 to 200 m²) to meet the growing demand for items 'made in Togo'.

For this department, the problem of supplies and raw materials has been resolved by what the Atelier Bon Conseil calls 'integral, direct recycling' – in other words, the collection of old parts and scrap metal in Togo and, above all, the receipt of metal tailings from European companies, such as Wild S.A. (Leica), Hilti, Forster, Jensen, Stanag and the Star Garage.

Joinery and Carpentry Department

Under the direction first of Christophe Sonderegger, who established it in 1983, and then of his brother Stephan, who took it over in 1987, this department produces windows, doors, ceilings, huts and coffering for a wide variety of customers, including the Centre's own Building Department.

The joiners manufacture a variety of solid wood furniture (chairs, tables and beds for instance) both for the home market and for export. Patterns are drawn up in the department and the objects are made in such woods as teak, iroko, mahogany or *franké*.

The department has a wide and varied range of customers who demand quality work and a choice of different styles. This means that the apprentices have the advantage of gaining experience in a wide variety of manufacturing, production and assembly techniques. As a result, they learn to prepare, handle, adjust and maintain all kinds of different machinery. Like the General Mechanics and Fitting Department, this department was enlarged in 1989 to attain its planned size of 306 m². The warehouse is managed by the apprentices themselves in spells of three months at a time. The Department employs a department head and three joiners. It has fifteen apprentices in various stages of training and also receives short-term trainees from the area who want to perfect their methods. A carpenter works under contract to the Centre and participates in the training of apprentices. There is a large warehouse for seasoning the large quantities of timber. This comes mainly from neighbouring Ghana, since the felling of trees is strictly controlled in Togo.

Locksmith and Welding Department

This department manufactures metal objects of every kind – railings, steel-plate cisterns, metal doors and gates – and it can handle any problem relating to locks or welding. The apprentices use the well-tried methods of arc-welding, with argon or carbon dioxide protection.

Street children work many hours in factories,
fields and mines for unscrupulous employers.
Photo: *ILO/J. Maillard*

Mechanical and
Electrical Car Fitting Department

his department handles every conceivable mechanical or electrical problem relating to light vehicles (cars and motorcycles).

Bodywork and Painting Department

The ten apprentices in this department, mainly concerned with repairing vehicles damaged in accidents or rusting from corrosion, also undertake bodywork modifications or accept orders to make bodywork 'to specification'.

Utility Vehicles Department

This department devotes its efforts to the repair and transformation of utility vehicles such as lorries, buses, tractors, specialized construction vehicles and agricultural machinery.

Building Department

This department provides, perhaps, the best illustration of the Centre's slogan: 'The impossible we achieve immediately; miracles take a little longer.' Some 90 per cent of the architectural plans are drawn up in the department and are handed over ready to use in accordance with the client's wishes. A wide assortment of undertakings is covered, ranging from the supply of a few simple breeze-blocks to complete individual houses or huts, water towers, bridges, flower gardens, tennis courts, canalizations, self-locking paving-stones, etc. The paving-stone machine produces 5,000 paving-stones a day. It was donated to the Centre by a concrete factory belonging to the German company Loech as an act of goodwill at Christmas.

It was the Building Department which constructed the entire Atelier Bon Conseil and this department generates the greater part of the Centre's turnover.

Refrigeration, Electricity and Plumbing Department

This department is responsible for repairing such items of electrical equipment as air-conditioners, household equipment, typewriters and other office machines. It also plays a major part in building construction and has done much to make the workshop known as a place where original solutions are found for special problems.

Transport and Goods Handling Department

Headed by the Assistant Manager of the Centre, Léon Djimeto Djossou, this department has two tip-lorries, a two-axle trailer, a caterpillar tractor, an air compressor and a water pump. All are used by the department but are, occasionally, rented out to outside customers. One of the lorries has been fitted with a lifting arm and is sometimes used as a crane.

Main Storehouse

The principle that nothing should be thrown away and the need for a permanent stock of materials underlines the great importance of the central storehouse. It is vital to be able to meet production needs, but also, as we have seen, for its pedagogical value.

Training a new generation of technicians

On average, 120 apprentices aged under 20, some of them girls, receive training in various crafts at the Centre over a four-year period. Some 50 other trainees (Togolese students or students from Burkina Faso, Côte d'Ivoire or Cameroon, who have completed their studies in Europe, and apprentices finishing their training in Togo) come to the centre each year for three to six months. They come on their own account or through organizations such as the Swiss Contact Foundation. They want to round off their theoretical and practical training. Each year the Centre receives 150 requests to participate in the competitive examination for the recruitment of apprentices but, unfortunately, it can only take the twenty best candidates.

The Atelier Bon Conseil is open to children who have dropped out of school, but the training programme does not include literacy or elementary education classes. Every effort is made to profit from previous schooling when teaching the apprentices the principles guiding each practical activity. Ideally the students are already up to the level of the *Brevet d'études élémentaires du premier cycle* (BEPC). This makes theoretical teaching easier but possession of this certificate, or of any other certificate for that matter, is not a prerequisite for entry to the Centre.

Divided into small groups, the students have eight hours of theoretical classes a week and thirty-two hours of practical training. The content of each of the theoretical courses (technology, mathematics, industrial design, physics, mechanics and electricity)

is based on the production work in progress in the different departments. The four years' training are rewarded by an apprenticeship
certificate, established and recognized by the state, and subject to
success in the final national examination.

Material help is given to the apprentices so that they can go
through their training under the best conditions. In Togo, it is
traditional for an apprentice to give a sum of money to the
artisan-teacher or to perform certain free services for him, in
return for training. The Atelier Bon Conseil, however, pays a
monthly bonus to apprentices who are considered to be
deserving, especially those who have given evidence of initiative,
creativity and productivity. This is why the practical training
sessions are always preceded by work involving constructive
imagination and individual projects. This enables the apprentice
to become aware both of the gaps in his education and his
aptitudes.

This kind of stock-taking is necessary since the objective of
the Atelier Bon Conseil is not only to give renewed hope of better
living conditions to young people in difficulty but also to play its
part in the creation of a new generation of technicians capable of
improvising machinery and who therefore know their own
aptitudes and limitations.

Success stories and extension plans

On completion of his or her training, it is essential to offer the
young apprentice an opportunity of insertion into active life:
otherwise training will have been a waste of time. For this
reason, several young artisans have received technical and
financial support from the Atelier Bon Conseil. The Centre takes

pride in two specific examples of success. In 1989, a former apprentice, who had become a fitter/mechanic, set up at Atakpame, the capital of a prefecture some 70 km from Kpalime. The Centre provided him with a second-hand lathe, which he himself had helped recondition. At present, this young craftsman is doing well and is gradually paying off the cost of repairing the lathe and installing his workshop. He himself is training two apprentices. The other young craftsman has set up in Bamako, Mali, and – a sure sign of success – has just built himself a villa at Kpalime.

Every former apprentice who sets up in business receives an advantageous loan and a study is being made on the feasibility of providing low-interest loans for apprentices' projects. Experience shows that only modest financial support for projects of this kind is needed to encourage the growth of craft trades in the country.

Young artisans can be reluctant to accept paid employment, but setting up on their own account is costly and limits the help the Centre can provide. In July 1990, in an attempt to remedy this situation, the Atelier Bon Conseil created the Association pour la Promotion de l'Artisanat au Togo at Agome-Kpalime in the hope of 'encouraging mutual assistance within the group and promoting the creation of artisanal businesses that could provide theoretical and practical training for apprentices in professional centres and establishments'. In addition, links were established with the Fonds National de l'Apprentissage et du Perfectionnement. Thanks to these links the Atelier Bon Conseil expects to receive a financial grant from the World Bank in 1994 for the training and insertion of young Togolese craftsmen into employment. This, however, will only meet half the annual training costs, estimated at $40,000.

Apart from the direct financial aid the Atelier Bon Conseil gives to apprentices, it also tries to create other conditions which would allow them to exercise their talents in various productive activities. The Joinery and Carpentry Department, for example, is about to move into the timber business; the Atelier Bon Conseil is negotiating the purchase of the Centre Artisanal d'Agou-Nyogbo, a former state sawmill situated 15 km from Kpalime. The new company, which will be independent, is to be called the Scierie et Menuiserie d'Agou-Nyogbo, Togo, or SMANTO. When it opens, its joinery section will be in a position to employ some fifty workmen and apprentices. The sawmill, which is the only one in the district, will supply wood both to its joinery section and to the Atelier Bon Conseil. It will also provide additional openings for employment and training. A third activity, in a factory, will be started for the production and treatment of electric cables. SMANTO will, of course, operate along the same principles as the Atelier Bon Conseil, that is, that nothing and nobody is to be wasted.

To establish its financial autonomy, SMANTO will seek to broaden the market for its products, in particular for furniture, to include the countries of the European Union. This will open up further opportunities for training in export and international trading techniques. To uphold these projects, and thanks to funding from Germany of DM.1.5 million, a forestation programme is being prepared. Thousands of hectares of land are being planted with a species of tree that will be exploitable in the medium to long term (ten to fifteen years and more). Thus, by broadening its range of action, the Atelier Bon Conseil is proving to be a venture of ever-growing importance to the country.

A two-pronged approach

The Atelier Bon Conseil is an innovative undertaking and there are many reasons for its success.

Its management capacity is solid and works on the principle of a minimum of administration for a maximum of production. Its strategy of quasi-autonomous funding means that the workshop has a chance of continuing when its original founders retire, an eventuality that has to be planned for.

Its horizons are not limited to the training of apprentices. It plays its part in their insertion into active life by a self-financing system. The graduate apprentices are seen as having a potential multiplier effect. They in turn could train new generations of competent, creative artisans.

By rehabilitating school drop-outs, the Atelier Bon Conseil provides a solution, if only on a modest scale, to the waste engendered by the formal education system. At the same time it helps prevent young people from falling into despair, delinquency and violence. The Centre's method of putting theory into the service of practice could be adopted as a pedagogical method in formal technical schools. In fact, the Centre already collaborates with the country's technical schools in putting the final touches to the pupils' practical training.

The Centre has demonstrated its interest in ecology and its concern for the environment ('There is a use for everything'). In June 1991, in Lomé, it set up the Association de Lutte Contre la Désertification de l'Afrique (ALCDA), whose objective is 'to encourage the plantation of forests, to promote the general awareness of their importance and train people in their upkeep and sustainable exploitation'.

The Centre's links with the population are both associative

and on a supplier/customer basis. The two-pronged approach it has adopted, of simultaneously conducting its training and commercial production activities, underlies all decisions made by the Centre and is undoubtedly one of its major assets. This approach seems to provide the best institutional formula for training technicians in general and artisans in particular. It is undoubtedly the most natural and the oldest method of instruction mankind has ever known. Human beings learned everything from their parents 'on the spot', and theory and practice were intermingled for centuries before the appearance of the collective education method we call school. This two-pronged approach is the most appropriate means of rehabilitating children who find themselves in difficulty, not because it is easier or less prestigious but rather because it meets a major psychological need in children of this category, namely, to learn and discover how to do something useful and beneficial to everyone and give oneself a feeling of positive worth.

The Atelier Bon Conseil appears to benefit everyone concerned – the founders, the apprentices and the general public (as customers). Since training takes place within the actual process of production and since the production output in itself has no pedagogical objective, the apprentices can be expected to develop a business sense. Furthermore, the output is subject to the scrutiny and sanction of customers, who will be using the products for specific purposes and results. In other words, the goods and services produced must correspond to the real needs of the market. This calls for effective management by the directors and, for the apprentices, a sense of responsibility for the quality, reliability and saleability of the product. The system also develops a sense of responsibility by using raw materials without excessive waste. The dual, self-financing approach means that the Centre cannot afford to allow the apprentices to take too large a margin for trial and error, all the more so, as the materials, as in laboratories of technical schools and universities, are very costly. Instructors and apprentices alike are obliged to make the workshop run in such a way that it will be permanently profitable for all.

On the other hand, there is a danger with the two-pronged approach that commercial preoccupations may take precedence over pedagogical objectives, which may be reduced to a minimum, or even disappear altogether, especially if commercial competition becomes too strong or self-financing becomes difficult to maintain. Commercial constraints may lead to the number of the apprentices being reduced to insignificance when viewed in terms of the number of young people in desperate need of training. Moreover, the educational and training content is undoubtedly the most costly – the time spent on theoretical classes eats into the time spent on actual production. Books and other pedagogical equipment, too, are not essential to production but have to be bought, external specialists employed to give certain complementary lessons have to be paid. There is, inevitably, a certain wastage of materials and damage to costly equipment, etc.

In a crisis, a purely commercial venture can declare itself bankrupt with no other problems than that of the loss of employment. An institution that has adopted the two-pronged approach cannot do this without also ruining all the hopes young people have placed in it. Psychological damage of this sort will be all the greater if it affects young people recovering from difficulties. On moral grounds, then, an institution adopting this two-pronged approach, whose value and effectiveness are recognized, must neither fail nor be abandoned. This is one of the founders' constant concerns at the Atelier Bon Conseil.

The bayaye *learn another trade*

Africa Foundation project, Kampala, Uganda

Kampala's orphans

Uncontrolled urbanization, prostitution, poverty: a number of such common causes can, obviously, be found for the abandoned children one comes across throughout Africa. Yet in each country, particular events have also played their part. In Uganda, one can point to the political, economic and social crisis precipitated by the Idi Amin dictatorship after 1971. First came the expulsion of the Indians, then the creation of artificial commercial activities to compensate. This impelled a good number of young people, then in school, to drop out and go after 'easy' money. After that came massacre or exile for thousands of opponents. And later still, after the dictator's fall, there was endless civil war.

In the 1970s, hundreds of orphans were wandering the streets of Kampala. Their average age was 8 to 10. They were called *bayaye,* meaning 'thieves'. Despite general indifference or even outright hostility and a total lack of action by the authorities, a handful of men and women shouldered the burden of looking after these children. One of these people was the Reverend Kefa Sempangi, creator of Africa Foundation.

Africa Foundation

As is the case with so many other non-governmental organizations working in this field, Africa Foundation is the result of one individual's initiative. Kefa Sempangi began taking care of a group of some thirty-five children in 1971. They were the offspring of single mothers, sometimes widows, incapable of meeting the cost of their children's schooling or even of their most basic needs. A number of these young were actually the children of vagabonds or even of physically or mentally handicapped parents. In 1973, Kefa Sempangi's work was interrupted by five years of exile. Upon his return in 1979, a number of parents came to see him again. So a small team came into being and Africa Foundation was born. Its goals: to shelter street children and abandoned youngsters and so readapt, train and reintegrate them into society. Since 1979, some 4,500 children have benefited from the project's activities. The project currently shelters some 1,500 children and gives them a formal or informal education. The headquarters are at Ddandira, Mukono district, some 15 km along the road from Kampala to Jinja. A staff of several dozen people handle administrative tasks or act as counsellors and teachers. At the top, management is ensured by a group of eight.

Although the number of street children and working children has been on the rise uninterruptedly over the last two decades, such has been the country's economic plight that Africa Foundation expected practically nothing by way of government support. Action had to be taken to overcome material obstacles difficult even to imagine in industrialized countries. The purchase of the equipment, needed to launch the project in 1979, was only made possible by a $30,000 grant from the Stichting Redt een Kind

(Help a Child) organization (Netherlands). This organization in fact continues to sponsor 320 children out of approximately 1,500. Africa Foundation receives roughly $18,000 a month from donors in Canada, Germany and Australia, but actually requires about $30,000 to meet the needs of its 1,180 non-sponsored children.

Further sources of funding and income had to be found. Australian donors provided $60,000, and a poultry-farming project was set up. In 1984, a further grant permitted the purchase of arable land for the breeding of goats (200 head at present) and pigs. In 1988, $3,000 helped start a tree-planting project. The children participated in all these activities. They not only became familiar with how to preserve the environment through agricultural activities, but learned how to take themselves in hand and so perceive the link between patient effort and patent result – and in so doing contribute to the financing of Africa Foundation.

Staged reintegration

The aim, then, is to take children off the streets, out of the markets and shanty-towns and to readapt them to a 'normal' way of life. But to do so, their trust must first be won, their basic needs met, their formal or informal education provided for, and their feelings of brotherhood or sisterhood aroused. They can, then, rediscover – or indeed discover – the very meaning of the word 'family'. The essence of Africa Foundation's education system lies in the realization that all these tasks cannot be tackled at once. These children come from a world ruled by its own norms and one can only take full account of this difference within a particular context and place. Such a place exists: it is the Katwe

Some 150 million children work in illegal,
dangerous, unhealthy conditions.
Photo: *UNICEF/Maggie Murray-Lee*

Centre, 3 km from the centre of Kampala. Here children are taken in when they arrive fresh off the street, slum or market-place. They are observed and encouraged. Efforts are made to discover their interests. Then they go on to further hostels, where they are oriented, according to their abilities and choice, towards job training or towards formal or informal education. The last stage is the 32-hectare Children's Village at Mukono.

There are stark variations between the levels of development and socialization among children just off the streets. Individual differences have to be spotted; some are due to natural factors but most stem from a particular environment. In most cases, a child's character will depend on the amount of time spent on the street and the persons frequented. This is why Africa Foundation provides different hostels for different groups, defined, as follows, during the children's first stay in the initial hostel. First, those who attended school for a time and then dropped out but who, given their age, can easily be reintegrated into a formal education system; second, those who have no education, but are beyond school age; third, those who have some schooling but who, given specific problems, can no longer go on with school; fourth, those aged approximately 15 with a bent for some manual activity: bricklaying, house-painting, etc. Given these criteria, along with those of age and sex, children first housed in the Katwe Centre are then directed towards one of the other hostels. There are two hostels at Mengo, in two buildings bought with an American grant in 1982. Fifty-five children are housed in each. The children here have received some formal schooling but with results too poor to go on to higher grades. Here they receive practical training in bricklaying, carpentry, electricity, etc. There are other hostels: Seguku, acquired in 1983, and Seeta. The latter takes in primary-school children who remain within a system of formal education. The Children's Village at Mukono is the last stage.

Mukono, acquired through an American grant, houses all those children who judging from their behaviour, attitudes and dealings with others are said to have, in effect, broken with their past way of life. The village here has six hostels where the children are housed, as well as the project's administrative office and two teaching centres, one where the children receive instruction from kindergarten level to the end of the primary cycle, and another where children who are too old for formal schooling receive vocational training.

No one at Mukono forgets that a child's life cannot be reduced to school activities. There are not only educational materials proper to each group but also indoor games (and television) and equipment for outdoor sports such as volley-ball and table tennis. But while Mukono is, as it were, the finishing point, the core of the whole project is the initial welcoming Centre at Katwe.

First steps are the most important: Katwe Centre

Katwe's situation – not far from the large market of Owino or from the shanty-town of Kisenyi, two areas where many street children live – is crucial to the project. Katwe shelters all those children ready to enter it, but it is not assumed that their decision to change their way of life is by any means a permanent one. Their numbers, therefore, vary continuously (on average between 100 and 250). One of the principal ideas of the entire project is that Katwe is where the decisive step is taken. Whatever level of education is reached later or whatever vocational training is received, the great victory is when the initial break is made. The decisive phase is the first phase.

From the outset, it is important that the material surroundings remain similar to those which the children have known up until then. The youngsters, therefore, first sleep on the floor on straw mats. After a month, perhaps sooner, they move to more comfortable rooms. But there is still a long way to go. 'It isn't easy', as Kefa Sempangi puts it, 'to change a marijuana joint into a glass of milk'.

Above all, it is patience that is needed. Dealing with street children is always difficult to start with. If their trust is to be secured they must be won over, for a period of about six months, by being provided with things which may command no particular priority in our eyes, but do enjoy undue priority in theirs. Give them a blanket and mattress, and they will sell them the next day. Repeat the process, and they will sell them again, and so on four or five times. Only then will they begin to perceive the importance of these objects; and then, should one refuse to provide any more, the children will return to the street or market.

One can immediately see how hard it is to draw up a budget or to foresee running expenses for the Centre, given its highly fluctuating population. In Africa Foundation's early days, objects and equipment were continually being looted or destroyed. The same item, occasionally, had to be bought four or five times in a row in one month.

The key role played by the initial centre is revealed in the fact that it is here that Africa Foundation keeps the bulk of its educational and recreational equipment. It should be recalled that children off the street need more leisure time than others.

They are provided with indoor games such as cards, scrabble and ludo, a television, etc. Katwe is close to the large shanty-town of Kisenyi. Children from this shanty-town spend some time at Katwe, even if they do not stay, and they then act as a ferment in the slums. The idea is to, almost, 'bait' them. It is only a starting-point, of course, but one which can prove effective. One project under consideration would consist of showing continuous educational videos in the common-room, though lack of resources has, so far, delayed this.

Here too, the children's specific interests are defined and their capacities sized up so that they can then be steered towards a literacy or basic arithmetic course. Accordingly, nearly all the available equipment for literacy instruction has been gathered together at Katwe – textbooks, instructors' manuals, flash cards and the like.

The Centre still needs a projector, a couple of televisions, two video cameras and other audiovisual equipment. The department which looks after basic arithmetic (which is combined with basic business studies) has five electric typewriters – twenty would be needed for its work to be truly effective.

Former street children help present street children

Among the counsellors at Katwe, as in the other hostels, are to be found former street children who have gone through all the project's various phases and now lead a so-called 'normal' life. Obviously enough, however, a permanent staff of professionals, from various fields, is also needed to manage the project's daily activities. Africa Foundation, therefore, has a governing board of eight persons, each qualified in a different field. It meets twice a month to oversee the project's functioning. One former street child is a board member and makes the children's voice heard there. He is Richard Nsubuga, a B.A. graduate in Business Administration from Syracuse University, New York. There is an accountant for the 'funding' department. The 'child care' department is headed by a sub-director responsible for co-ordinating social workers and teachers, from both the formal and informal sectors. This department also drafts social and educational plans of action.

Nothing, however, would be possible without the participation of those now 'readapted' youngsters who were on the street themselves and have personally experienced the different phases in the readaptation process. They are the ones who supply the social workers and other adults with the relevant and vital information needed to approach street children for the first time, and they continue to provide invaluable help to children passing from one phase to the next. Their experience is irreplaceable; they know these children better than anyone else; they understand their motives because these motives were once their own; they realize how far work or formal education can be removed from these youngsters' initial concerns – they know the story of Geoffrey Sserwada, who graduated from Makerere University in June 1992. He confessed one day to Kefa Sempangi that he had first shown up at the Centre in 1979 pretending to want to change his life and become a chauffeur. Certainly he wanted to learn to drive cars, but only so that he could steal them!

All the youngsters take part in the continual decision-making, from determining how to use the funds supplied by sponsoring donors to drawing up menus or deciding how to dress. They also help in other ways such as cleaning rooms, washing dishes, farming and stock-raising. In all cases, the aim is to instil a sense of responsibility by having the children assume their own share of the burden at all levels.

The children's participation also follows more 'official' lines. From initial Centre to final Village, the youngsters choose those who will represent them on the hostel management committees. From the very outset, these committees, in turn, help discover each child's abilities and decide on his or her future course. These children are better placed than anyone to understand the language of their own peers, their dress habits and the like, and to give advice to those youngsters who have not yet given up marijuana, solvent-sniffing or stealing. In a word, children help other children successfully through their initial transformation – without which nothing else would be possible.

The results

Few of the children first arriving at Katwe think in terms of a formal education or even of any kind of vocational training. In general, they are looking for shelter, temporary or not. Still, despite this absence of motivation – or despite their contradictory motivations – these children must be given an education if their social reintegration is to succeed at all, otherwise the whole project would be no more than a breathing space between two periods of degradation.

The most important effort here concerns literacy. Roughly 50 per cent of the 4,500 children who benefited from the project started out illiterate. Between 1979 and 1984, Africa Foundation taught about 2,000 children how to read. Some adolescents joined the project after as much as twelve years of street life. It was extremely difficult for them to visualize life with a 'real' and stable job with rigid constraints. What the project was able to do was offer them literacy, thereby leaving the door open. Some 2,225 youngsters aged 18 or over grabbed this opportunity and now carry out small trades as outdoor vendors, car washers, etc. They escaped delinquency.

At the other end of the scale lies university education. Despite their handicaps and the enormous attendant hurdles, several dozen children from Africa Foundation have managed to obtain university degrees in Uganda or the United States. In addition, 5.8 per cent of the readapted children have secured degrees or certificates in higher education: 250 youngsters have thus qualified as accountants, secretaries, nurses, engineers or teachers. The main effort has, nevertheless, been in the field of vocational training. Out of 4,500 children, 1,775 have learned a trade and some have become carpenters and joiners (500), electricians (55), tailors (80) and launderers (40); about 100 youngsters have received training in various forms of agricultural activity. 1,000 young people have learned various forms of craftsmanship or applied arts: painting and interior decoration (350), ceramics and pottery (150), wood-carving (25), mat- and carpet-weaving (400), and leatherwork and shoemaking (75).

Out of the 4,500 children or adolescents who have benefited from the project, it is fair to say that 90 per cent have escaped the street. But each youngster has stayed a average of twelve years with Africa Foundation. In Kampala, the number of street children is growing daily, in some cases due to reasons outside the jurisdiction of Uganda, others linked to the country's recent past, and yet others common to all African societies.

There is a direct link between the lack of education prospects and the presence of children on the street. According to the 1980 *Education Policy Review Report,* 52 per cent of Ugandans aged 18 or over were illiterate. In 1990, 75 per cent of those who had completed their primary education were unable to go on to a higher level. A project such as Africa Foundation is powerless, of course, to deal with social problems of this scale. What is the Foundation to do about uninterrupted migration to the cities, proliferating shanty-towns, growing poverty, and the spread of prostitution? But each child saved provides a ferment for change. And even one child saved makes all efforts worth while.

Gamines *of Medellín*

The Ciudad Don Bosco project, Medellín, Colombia

'Medellín, the damned' ran a headline in the French newspaper *Le Monde* a few years ago. In many ways a town like any other, Medellín would undoubtedly prefer to make the headlines less often. The acute violence found there is only a particularly spectacular form of the endemic brutality that afflicts that part of South America. The same poverty and the same destitute children are to be found elsewhere.

However, there is one difference. The Salesian order (founded by the nineteenth-century Italian saint and pioneer of service to street children, Don Bosco), established the Ciudad Don Bosco project and has acquired over the years a remarkable wealth of experience in helping the working and street children of Medellín.

As early as 1915, a night centre opened in Medellín for shoeshine boys and young newspaper vendors. A primary school and a small dispensary were added in 1956. In 1960, the city of Medellín provided plots of land at Robledo–Barrio Aures, to the north-west of the city, and in 1972 the various services moved there. By December 1992, there were 567 children and adolescents participating in the project. Among them, 147 teenagers aged 15 to 19 were involved in the Social Development Programme.

The Ciudad Don Bosco buildings are situated in one of the roughest areas of the city. In these areas, unemployment is rife, public services are almost non-existent and the housing situation is terrible. The only conceivable 'future' for many teenagers is membership of a gang of petty criminals or even of a group of *sicarios,* the drug barons' 'tough guys'.

It is, therefore, not surprising that, in Medellín, there are many cases of abandoned or runaway children. The worst cases are those of the vagrant children who roam around in gangs, surviving on a hand-to-mouth basis, often by begging and theft. Ciudad Don Bosco does its best to help them and there is no discrimination between the various categories of children or adolescent in difficulty. Street vagrants, abandoned children, unemployed youths, young pre-delinquents – all are welcome at Ciudad Don Bosco.

Some children are sent by the Instituto Colombiano de Bienestar Familiar (ICBF), a Colombian public institution for the protection of children in distress, which makes a sizeable contribution to the project. ICBF is not the only source of funds. Part of the funding comes from the Salesian order itself. Self-financing, through various workshops, also plays a substantial role. Finally, many Colombian and foreign donors support the project. Nevertheless, as with other organizations pursuing the same goals, ever-growing needs mean that finances are a constant source of worry for Ciudad Don Bosco.

The immediate aim of the project is to achieve the reintegration of the child or adolescent into the family and the wider community through education and practical training. On a wider scale, the goal is to produce responsible citizens. Ever since its creation in the nineteenth century and wherever it has operated in the world, the Salesian order has considered work

Non-formal education to fight exclusion.
Photo: *Kimmo Kosonen*

– more precisely practical training – to be the fundamental way of getting young people off the streets.

Wider educational and philosophical concepts underpin this direction. Ciudad Don Bosco does not set out to be just a welfare or training centre; its target is rather the overall development of the children through a slow and lengthy process which has its own specific rhythm of progression and regression, of ups and downs. The organizers' commitment is overtly religious – Ciudad Don Bosco intends to produce not only active citizens but also good Christians. However, in the short and medium term, modification of the children's behaviour is sought through immediate and realistic objectives.

The first step is to establish contact with the children and to win their confidence. Twice a week, at night, the organizers of the project and helpers from ICBF go out to visit the street children. At first, the sharing of a few cigarettes or sweets and a simple 'Hi there' are sufficient. Little by little, the adults try to entice the children to come to the Patio del Gamin, a welfare centre situated near the buildings of Ciudad Don Bosco. Here, the basic needs of food, medical care, games and sport and permanent dialogue can be satisfied.

Once this stage is completed, the child enters the 'transition centre', the first centre of the Ciudad Don Bosco complex. Some thirty children are accommodated there every six months. At the centre they can enjoy decent accommodation and are prepared for future activities such as literacy training, manual work and various cultural activities. Here the aim is to break with past habits that constituted their daily round – theft, drugs, sexual promiscuity and violence. This is also the stage when the educators attempt to form an initial assessment of each child and to determine his or her needs and potential.

The third so-called 'protection and assistance' phase concerns an average of 180 children (aged 11 to 17) plus about 130 children who are weekly boarders. This phase does not represent a radical break with the preceding stage, but rather a redirection in the fields of education, work or cultural activities.

The 'training centre' (fourth phase) caters for around 190 children aged 15 to 18. While receiving academic schooling appropriate to their age-group (study for the Colombian baccalaureate), the children also receive instruction in a variety of practical trades: metalwork, needlework, electricity, carpentry and lithography. The adolescents 'learn as they produce' and receive an income in one form or another. They enter directly into the world of work, and this is considered to be the main way of bringing about a transformation in their personalities.

The 'residence' (fifth phase) houses fifty adolescents, aged 15 to 18, selected according to their abilities and interests. A system of scholarships enables them to attend various schools in Medellín. They are involved not only in the running of the different aspects of daily life at the residence but also in devising and managing varying facets of the project rules, content and orientation of training, etc.

Finally, the 'mini-workshops' are more a separate experience than a particular phase of the project since at present they involve only about a dozen adolescents. They consist of between six and twelve mini-businesses, spread out in various areas of Medellín, operating under the general supervision of a project co-ordinator for the training centre (electricity, woodwork, etc.). Through a system of monthly payments, the trainees, who must be aged over 17, can eventually become the owners of their workshops.

The Social Development Programme

This programme, which at present involves some 150 weekly boarders aged 15 to 24 (66 per cent of whom are boys), provides practical training for adolescents who have not broken all links with their families but who are 'in distress'. In Colombia, this tends to mean young people who: (a) are unemployed; (b) have dropped out of school and have had no practical training; (c) are victims of a particularly difficult family situation (extreme poverty, absent father or mother); and (d) belong to gangs, have taken drugs and can broadly be categorized as pre-delinquents. These young people receive practical training in the workshops of the Ciudad Don Bosco Training Centre in the same trades as the other adolescents at the centre: metalwork, needlework, etc. The fundamental principle is summed up in the centre's motto: 'Learn as you produce.'

The youngsters can join one of the programme's teams in February, June or September. The minimum duration of the courses is four months; however, those who wish to do so can stay on longer. Work lasts thirty to forty-five hours a week, from Monday to Saturday.

The Social Development Programme works for several companies in the city. The young people receive an income based on the instructors' evaluation of their work. They are assessed on a 1-to-10 scale that takes into account their use of raw materials, the skills they demonstrate and their ability to communicate with their companions and instructors. Some of the trainees also spend short, paid periods of training in certain client companies.

A support team, consisting of a doctor, a psychologist, a social worker and a priest, is available to the trainees. It does its best to see to all those problems that are not strictly related to their training.

The aim of this programme, in fact, is not just to offer these young people the opportunity of escaping unemployment and delinquency by practical training and the possibility of future employment; it also tries to bring about a change in their behavioural patterns and their values through work and the acquisition of a spirit of co-operation and collective effort.

Part Three

Using the street

The idea of using the street should, in no way, be seen as a defeatist acceptance of the problem of street children. It is not a means of keeping the child on the street or a means of controlling the phenomenon. It is rather a way of turning the street into a positive entity and not into a negative failure. Any child brought up on the street will have suffered in some way, but these projects, rather than reject the past, try to capitalize on the street children's experience which gives them practical intelligence, boldness and a desire to survive. The solutions lie in the hands of the urban poor and the street children themselves. It is this force and power which can and should be harnessed to stimulate the children into action.

First, one must create a sense of action out of the children's constant and pressing aim to survive. They confront dangers and obstacles every day, and their education and training are further hurdles that can be overcome with the same determination that drives a child to carry on, day after day, despite the odds. The HLM Montagne Project in Senegal creates a positive environment out of a slum. The founders have turned a shack into a school, organized training activities, a theatre group, sewing classes and a real centre of activity. The street has been made to work. People have turned their situation to profit, not succumbed.

In India at the Bosco Project, the street has been made to produce positive results in the face of dire poverty. The rag-pickers used barely to survive on their scavenging activities; now they are organized within a co-operative and are assured of an income and protection. The power for change lies within the community. At the Paaralang Pang-tao Project the squatters and street children have successfully restructured a dumpsite, made a school and established a training and theatre workshop. Through acting, recycling and lessons the dumpsite is no longer a source of despair but an inspiration. Out of nothing has come satisfaction and production.

Survival
through learning

Centre for domestic servants
in the HLM Montagne quarter of Dakar, Senegal

ENDA Jeunesse-Action was formed in 1985 following a forum held at Grand-Bassam, Côte d'Ivoire. Groups have been established at Bamako (Mali), Dakar and Ziguinchor (Senegal), and the ENDA Jeunesse-Action programme has been adopted by a number of groups operating independently in Cotonou (Benin) and Saint-Louis (Senegal). The ENDA Jeunesse-Action team has set itself two objectives: to encourage exchanges between groups helping street children, both in Africa and other continents (through regional training workshops and by publishing and disseminating information and knowledge); and to give direct support to existing projects helping street children. (See box on page 209 for methodology and group philosophy.)

In Dakar, ENDA Jeunesse-Action helps over seventy distinct projects for children and young people. It works through sporting and cultural associations as well as with children and youths carrying out odd jobs such as shining shoes, refilling throwaway lighters, and washing and guarding cars. It works alongside children who have broken with their families and those who roam around in gangs in the market-places, cinemas and on the beaches. It is also involved with girls and young women in difficulty (school drop-outs and girls working as domestic servants). This account concerns the latter.

Working as a housemaid – a dog's life

HLM[1] Montagne, Dakar, is one of those mushroom districts that have sprung up on the fringes of all the great megapolitan areas of the world. The waste ground around these low-rent housing areas of Dakar is now illegally occupied by squatters who live in ramshackle dwellings made out of recovered corrugated iron and cardboard cartons. There are a few properly constructed houses, but the rent they command puts them out of reach of the majority of the local population. There is no electricity supply or drainage system. Nevertheless, the area's micro-economy includes a number of mechanical workshops, smithies and small trading establishments. At the far end of the district a few small and medium-sized businesses survive with difficulty.

Like most slums of its kind, HLM Montagne is an area for rural immigrants. Driven to the city by the severe droughts affecting their homelands, they come in the hope of earning enough to help support their families back in the villages. What differentiates HLM Montagne from other similar districts, however, is the large concentration of *mbindaan*, or housemaids.

These are young girls of the Serer people, an ethnic group from central Senegal. Aged 10 to 21, for the most part illiterate and speaking Wolof (one of the main national languages of Senegal), they work as domestic servants. Dakar, however, is hardly the Eldorado of their dreams. Far from their roots and

---

1. HLM (*habitation à loyer modéré*): low-rent housing.

familiar surroundings, these girls find themselves faced with many problems.

To solve the accommodation problem, groups of friends, or girls from the same village, club together to rent rooms. They live several to a room of 10–12 m², in shacks with no drinking water, electricity or drainage. Nevertheless, they manage to remain well organized and maintain a sense of solidarity, taking care of girls who have not yet found – or who have lost – jobs.

The process of looking for a job begins with a laborious door-to-door search. As they have neither professional training nor schooling, the girls usually try to find a place with an urban family where they can fulfil those domestic tasks to which all Senegalese girls are initiated from a tender age.

They have no qualifications, no experience of urban life and are available in very large numbers. They are obliged, therefore, to accept the conditions imposed upon them (very low wages and no guarantee of stable employment). Their employers themselves often have very modest and fluctuating incomes. As a result, there are frequent disputes about the tasks they are asked to do and the hours they are supposed to work. They are engaged by verbal contract only and this can be broken at any time by the employers when they want to rid themselves of a domestic. Employers are ready to put forward any pretext – incompetence, theft, repeated late arrival and long absence, even when due to illness. Furthermore, female domestics are often subjected to sexual assault by the sons of the family, if not by the head of the household himself.

With the rare exception of those who benefit from official regulations, applied only to expatriate households, these domestic servants are not covered by their employers for social security purposes and do not themselves contribute to any social security system. To add to all the nuisances of urban life, they are exposed to considerable health problems, including unwanted pregnancies and sexually transmissible diseases. Last but not least, they are likely to live on a far from balanced diet. With luck, when they return home in the evening, they may bring a bowl of food saved from the midday meal. This is shared with all the other occupants of their room.

Dressmaking skills and literacy

In 1984, ENDA Tiers Monde and the Ministry for Social Development launched a joint programme to improve the lot of young domestic servants living in the HLM Montagne district. A family education adviser got to know the young girls and women of the HLM Montagne district and after several months of contact a number of measures were taken.

The first of these, the creation of a centre, was designed to meet one of the basic requests of the girls themselves. Since their rooms were too small for ten to twenty girls to gather in, they wanted a place where they could get together to discuss their lives and problems. The HLM Montagne centre met this need, but it also went further by becoming a place where they could receive the instruction they desperately needed and wanted.

Realizing that on-the-job apprenticeships in the minor crafts (carpentry, masonry, etc.) were reserved for men, the girls looked for activities within their scope. They opted for courses in crochet-work, dressmaking and knitting, with a view to training for their future duties as mothers and housewives, and as a way to learn a craft. In the short term, they saw this as a means of earning additional income by selling items to their employers. In the longer term, they thought that they could pass on what they had learned to their younger sisters, thereby enabling them to remain in their villages.

A general-purpose room equipped with tables, benches, a blackboard and a cupboard was placed at their disposal. The girls took it in turns to clean and maintain the room.

Courses in crocheting, dressmaking and knitting were organized. These last three years and are divided into two sections according to the availability of those taking part. Evening classes are given three nights a week, between 8 and 10 p.m., for those working in town as domestic servants during the day. At present sixty-nine girls attend these classes. Afternoon classes (two hours) are given daily from Monday to Friday for young school drop-outs, aged 14 to 18. They live in the district and often work at home preparing the midday meal and doing the housework. Twenty-two of them attend these classes. The first year is devoted to introductory training (the first steps in stitching, making small-scale items and how to set about creating a garment), the second to the making of full-size garments (bodices, underwear, dresses and shirts) and the third to the consolidation and broadening of the skills acquired. In addition, cooking lessons are periodically organized for the girls.

The language during these courses is Wolof. The girls themselves provide the educational materials (wool and pieces of cloth) and they decide on the types of objects to be made for sale. They consider the needs and tastes of the city-dwelling Senegalese families they know. Assessment of the girls' work is simple and practical. The test at the end of the first year consists of being able to produce a garment on a miniature scale.

An element of literacy teaching is associated with this course.

This literacy training lasts the same time as the other courses and is designed to address the objectives the girls have set for themselves. Their two free weekday evenings, therefore, are devoted to literacy training. The aim is to be able to: (a) introduce friends, i.e. give their first names, surnames, address, the names of their parents and their profession; (b) explain, in French, what they are learning at the centre in dressmaking, crochet-work, knitting and cooking; (c) read and write about the tools and materials they use in their work; and (d) keep simple accounts and manage a family budget. The girls working as domestic servants consider that literacy classes will increase their chances of being employed by expatriate or well-to-do families who pay higher wages.

Generally speaking, the young girls of the district who have dropped out of school have a different goal. Their aim is to obtain the elementary school-leaving certificate. The literacy classes for these girls are held in the morning and are designed primarily to bring them up to the normal level and/or to consolidate knowledge already acquired. This means they can take the examination for the certificate of completion in primary studies or even the one giving them access to the first level of secondary education.

The pedagogical material used consists of books on reading and writing, in French, drawn up by a national education institution. There is further teaching material produced by the literacy network of the Martin Luther King UNESCO Club, a training body associated with ENDA Jeunesse-Action.

At the beginning, there is no individual counselling in the formal sense of the term; instead there is just an informal discussion. The girls are then directed towards the literacy classes where necessary and/or to the first or second year of dressmaking,

Young girl selling cigarettes in the street;
taking on small jobs can often be the only means
of survival for the child and his or her family.
Photo: *Bahay Tuluyan*

knitting and crochet-work. A monthly literacy assessment is made, both orally and in writing. No proficiency certificates are given at the end of the course, but this is simply because, so far, the girls have not expressed a desire or need for them.

The young women prove the high value they place on these courses in two ways. Firstly, with mere wages of 4,000 to 10,000 CFA francs, they do not hesitate to pay the 500 CFA francs they have to contribute towards the courses. Secondly, their persistence and assiduity are equally revealing. After working very long hours (ten to twelve hours, sometimes more, each day) and walking several kilometres to return to their district, the girls still have the energy and the will-power to attend evening courses, clean and maintain the centre, and look after teaching materials. This is true throughout the year except for certain particular times of religious or family celebrations.

The girls are genuinely and profoundly motivated. It is hardly surprising then that their acquisition of dressmaking, knitting and crochet-work skills is so rapid and that very often their progress towards literacy is truly satisfactory.

Some of the women abandon the courses when they change district or are housed with their employers, either of which makes it very difficult for them to maintain contact with the centre.

Meeting other needs

Training and education – while essential to these young girls if they are to be given proper means to cope with their major problems – are not everything. So the HLM Montagne centre offers them other activities.

The girls go on outings to discover the capital and its sites, such as the Island of Gorée (notorious as the dispatch point for the slave trade). They request showings of educational films and have established their own theatre group, which puts on performances in various districts. They can act out the realities of their daily lives, breaking out of their isolation and making themselves known in the area.

These leisure moments are an extremely important means of relaxation for these girls suffering from great stress. Chat sessions are sometimes organized, at the girls' demand. The discussion often hinges on the dangers that threaten them in the city. The centre staff and medically qualified guest speakers, invited by the girls themselves, talk about AIDS, other sexually transmitted diseases, clandestine abortion, the health of mother and child, and the nutritional follow-up of children from birth to 5 years.

This last subject arises because employers do not allow domestic servants to bring their children to work with them. Mothers working as domestic servants are obliged to leave their infants at home. They normally leave them in the care of very young girls. In the course of their home visits, the centre staff had noticed that many of these infants were suffering from malnutrition and various other illnesses. As a result, vaccination sessions were organized and a series of cookery demonstrations were arranged to show how, by using locally available cereals, the young mothers could give their children a low-cost balanced diet.

In 1988, the centre set up a catering facility in order to: (a) create an economically viable activity; (b) enable domestics, not fed at their workplace, to have a balanced, inexpensive meal; (c) give those working in the catering group additional training in nutritional balance, food hygiene and the conservation of food; and (d) round off training by teaching European-style menus so that the trainees have a greater chance of employment with European families. Subsequently, the restaurant, or *gargote* (nosh shop) as it was affectionately called, developed a life and a history of its own. Most of the initial young women, once they had established the restaurant as a self-financing unit, returned to their villages. The *gargote,* however, did not produce a sufficient profit to meet the needs of all the young girls at the centre. It carries on, therefore with a smaller staff of three girls.

Staff encouragement and motivation (the key)

The young domestics' motivation and determination is strengthened by the staff's attitude. The team in particular encourages the girls to discuss and determine the programme with them. Neither the permanent staff nor those occasionally involved set themselves up as 'masters' or 'mistresses' but as men and women who are able to communicate with young people in difficult situations. They see their role as being that of friendly advisers, encouraging young people to find their own road to self-fulfilment.

The centre's activities involve the direct participation of two female instructors in home economics, aged 40 and 45, both graduates of the National School for the Training of (Female) Home Economics Advisers and both of whom receive supplementary payment from ENDA, in addition to the regular pay they get from the Ministry; one part-time female instructor, aged 27, who receives 15,000 CFA francs from ENDA and 15,000 CFA francs from the students' contributions; and two voluntary literacy workers, aged 35 and 25, who receive 35,000 and 10,000 CFA francs, respectively, for their transport expenses. The advisers also have some pedagogical background thanks to the ENDA Jeunesse-Action training sessions and the regular experience-sharing meetings. Since 1992, there has also been a Consultative Committee to exchange views with instructors from other towns.

Maintaining links with the home village

The domestics living at HLM Montagne maintain links with their home villages and are kept in touch through new arrivals. Although the wages they earn are insufficient for them to make substantial savings, the money gained in the city enables them to help support their families in the villages, to prepare a marriage trousseau and to pay their contribution to their village associations.

This small-scale saving enables them to envisage some means of reinsertion into the village economy, even though at times

---

A participatory methodology

ENDA does not, in fact, see itself as a funding agency. Its regional training programme on research/action clearly propounds the need for beneficiaries to play the leading role in their own development. All this involves discussion with the different groups concerned and their participation. The young and the instructors determine all activities undertaken together. Delegates from the child and youth groups join in the annual elaboration of the team's future orientations. In the same way, the team has broadened its partnership with state organizations so as to reach all those involved.

The activities the ENDA Jeunesse-Action team has undertaken, in Dakar, on behalf of young girls in difficulty are having a knock-on effect. New activities, such as the two described below, are coming into being.

The 'petites bonnes' of the Rail district

A number of young house servants, aged 8 to 13, live in a district of Dakar known as the Rail. These young girls, who have never attended school, made it known that they wanted to learn to read and write. With the backing of ENDA Tiers Monde, twenty girls have been able to attend literacy courses. A token contribution of 20 CFA francs is asked for. The courses are given by a voluntary teacher who is a member of one of the district associations. Classes last two hours and are held three times a week. They take place in a shack, measuring 4 m^2, which is lent to them by 'the big girls'. The ENDA Jeunesse-Action team provides support in the form of books, pictures, etc. At present, the girls are trying to find a more spacious room in the district.

The domestic servants of Niayes Tioker (Reubeuss)

Fifteen domestic servants living in the Niayes Tioker district approached the ENDA Jeunesse-Action team with a request for literacy classes. The major difficulty was finding suitable premises in the district. As they lived near the Isaac Forster secondary school, where classes for porters from the Kermel market were already being held, it was decided to create a combined, mixed class for the girls and the porters.

The 8 p.m. timing of the classes suited both the porters and the domestics; however, the same was not true for the contents of the course since the needs and concerns of the two groups diverged. The porters, in particular, want be able to speak to their clients, most of whom are expatriates, in French. Some have even requested a literacy course in English as they often come into contact with English-speaking tourists. Altogether fifteen literacy instructors, most of them voluntary, are working in the district with the women, children and young people. Some of them have been trained by the Dakar Community Literacy Network.

---

drought and impoverishment renders living conditions there too precarious to hope to return. Nevertheless, most girls continue to long for their home village. A group of young girls from the village of Ngoye Alioune Sylla (Bambey department) succeeded in establishing activities such as sheep-raising and dyeing in their village. Similarly, contact is maintained with domestic servants looking for work opportunities in their home village of Karttiack, in the Ziguinchor region. The hostilities currently affecting this region, however, mean that any hopes of return are temporarily blocked.

In fact, projects where income-generating schemes are set up in the home villages offer the possibility of economic development and social advance in rural areas. The projects are, furthermore, a means of stemming the rural exodus.

Meanwhile, through its range of activities, the Centre makes a considerable impact on its immediate surroundings and on neighbouring districts. As already mentioned, the young girls of the district who have dropped out of school can also take advantage of the centre's training facilities. The nutritional follow-up sessions for infants under 5 are not restricted to young domestics but are attended by many (more than 80 per cent) of women of the district. The chat sessions and film shows are also keenly attended by the people of the district and, finally, the performances put on by the domestics' theatrical group have allowed them to establish a communication with the local population. All this has led to a breaking down of barriers and enabled the young domestics to make new friends outside their village circle. They are invited to family occasions, such as weddings and baptisms, and to other events in the district. Almost in spite of themselves, their integration into the urban milieu progresses step by step.

ENDA Jeunesse-Action has had to pay a price for its success. It receives a constant stream of requests for similar action in other districts where women face similar problems and conditions. (See box on page 210.)

To determine their needs and ensure the necessary follow-up, an inquiry into domestic servants is being undertaken in conjunction with the International Labour Organization (ILO) and the United Nations Children's Fund (UNICEF) in the Dakar area. The qualitative aspect of this inquiry has been entrusted to ENDA Tiers Monde, in collaboration with its Jeunesse-Action team. Research/action activities are being undertaken by the 'petites bonnes' (see box on page 210) to this end. The results of the inquiry will lead to a better understanding of this section of the population and enable existing contacts to spread further.

The Bosco kids of Bangalore

Bosco Yuvodaya street children project, Bangalore, India

It is estimated that some 45,000 children live on the streets of Bangalore, a figure which increases every day. For these children the street is their only home (many of them were actually born on the pavements of the city); it is the place where they eat, sleep, earn their living and grow up and where 'street wisdom' is the only form of education. About 80 per cent of these children are boys, since girls do not survive on the streets for long. Girls over the age of 12, found on the streets, are often engaged in prostitution.

The vast majority of children followed up by Bosco are boys aged between 12 and 18. Most eke out a precarious living collecting waste paper and rags, hawking and vending, or working as shoeshine boys, porters and car-park attendants. For many of these street children, Bosco is a beacon of hope in their dark despair.

What is Bosco?

Bosco was initiated as a part-time venture in June 1980 by a group of students from Kristu Jyothi College, Bangalore. In 1984, a full-time team was formed and the venture has grown to become one of the largest and most comprehensive projects for street children in India.

'Bosco' stands for Bangalore Oniyavara Seva Coota, which translates from Kannada (one of the major languages of south-western India) as 'an association of those who serve the people of the street'.

It also draws inspiration from Don Bosco, the nineteenth-century Italian saint who was a pioneer in serving the street children of Turin and founder of the Society of St Francis de Sales (the Salesians of Don Bosco).

Objectives

- To assist each street youngster to cope with life on the street, to take advantage of the street situation and of opportunities that may present themselves, and to assimilate these experiences so as to change into a well-rounded individual.
- To help street children become aware of their potential as individuals.
- To create and provide suitable environments that will allow for their total development.
- To provide a holistic concept of growth and education.
- To act as a catalyst that will challenge and change the existing education and socio-political systems, to provide an effective, viable alternative for the deprived.
- To facilitate debate and to move towards a new, improved education system.

These objectives have been given concrete expression in definitive action plans that are now operational. This has been achieved by:

- Identifying areas where street children are concentrated and providing a team of educationists to assist them and create a climate of growth on the street.
- Making use of the street and helping to make it a growth-oriented rather than an exploitative environment (for example, through the street-presence initiative described below).
- Creating and organizing programmes and services that will enhance the children's belief in themselves and their abilities (including counselling and anti-addiction programmes, medical and health components, orientation programmes, camps, street classes, advocacy and protection, advice on savings, solid waste management, etc.).

Community involvement

Bosco has developed as a community-based project involving society at large and using the services available within the community. This involves identifying the measure of responsibility of every member of the community for the growth and development of each street child and for the prevention of delinquency, truancy and other related problems.

This is achieved by action at different levels:

- At the city level, Bosco collaborates with the Action Committee of Governmental and Non-governmental Organizations, with the city corporation, government departments for home, woman and child, education, youth services and labour, and a variety of non-governmental organizations. Bosco is also the animating force behind the Bangalore Forum for Street and Working Children in which a number of individual citizens, youth clubs and other institutions participate.

- On a larger scale, Bosco operates in conjunction with the National Forum, the Justice Forum and with every organization that works for policy implementation and transformation.
- Bosco closely follows national and state educational policy, legislation on juvenile justice and child labour, as well as public awareness and the media.
- Local rallies, national campaigns and policy-oriented or issue-based struggles are transforming Bosco into a nationwide movement.
- Consultations at the national level as well as local level studies and experiments are now being undertaken with the aim of providing an alternative education system.

Today

We are guilty of so many errors and many faults.
But our worst crime is abandoning the children,
Neglecting the fountain of life.
Many of the things we need can wait, the child cannot.
Right now is the time.
His bones are being formed,
His blood is being made
And his senses are being developed.
To him we cannot answer 'Tomorrow'.
His name is 'Today'.

Gabriela Mistral

Buddhivantha

Buddhivantha, the name given to Bosco's innovative educational programme, is a common word in Kannada – a Dravidian language widely used in south-western India. It has Sanskrit roots and is deeply rooted in the Indian cultural ethos, but does not translate easily.

A delinquent youngster, or anyone who makes mistakes which have a lasting influence on his life, is often called *Buddhi kettoithu*, i.e. one who has lost his *Buddhi*.

Equally, when someone turns over a new leaf, achieves definite progress or accomplishes a spectacular feat, he is called *Buddhivantha*, which might be translated as 'one who has come to his senses, who is wise, who knows the difference between good and evil'. A *Buddhivantha* is someone who has the inner know-how to manage life and people. All this and more is implied in the word *'Buddhivantha'*.

The great sage Buddha was given that title because he was 'the Enlightened'.

Recalling this will help us to understand the deeper dimension of *Buddhivantha* as an educational concept.

To become a Buddha is considered to be an exclusive preserve, the prerogative of a few. To be a *Buddhivantha*, however, is a possibility open to anyone and is used in common language to denote the achievements of the ordinary man.

In the traditional village setting, the honorific *'Buddhi'* is used to address the elders and is in some ways comparable to the English 'sir'.

There is a distinction, however. The use of 'sir' tends to indicate someone's rank or position, whereas *'Buddhi'* is used to address one who is wise and has the wisdom that comes from experience and age.

The Buddhivantha education programme hopes to help youngsters, especially street children, to achieve integration and happiness in life.

Buddhivantha is Bosco's educational philosophy.

Uncontrolled urban growth creates slums,
deserted areas, polluted wastelands. City services are slow in coping.
Photo: *UNICEF*

Making and maintaining contact

At any one time, Bosco is in contact with about 2,000 of the estimated 45,000 street children in Bangalore.

The Bosco approach is based on 'being present with the young in all possible circumstances'. The contact staff operate mainly in areas where the children tend to congregate – at the bus station, the railway station and the markets. They maintain a constant vigil and try to meet every child who ends up on the street.

Street presence

This constant 'street presence' is the keystone of the Bosco method – the street is where the problem is and that is where it must first be tackled. The mere presence of caring Bosco staff on the streets is the beginning of the street child's education. There is no selection process as such and there is no drop-out rate either.

Every child on the street in the Bosco target areas is contacted and followed up. After a minimum of three months on the streets, children who participate with the educators in their process of growth and development progress to the Buddhivantha educational follow-up (see box on page 217). Buddhivantha is not specifically institution-based. Although children may be directed to one of many community institutions for specific instruction, this is only a phase in their development and growth, and if they find a particular phase inadequate or unsuited to them, they may opt out. Other modes of growth and development will open out.

This does not mean that there are no failures. On the contrary, there are bound to be setbacks in each child's progress and development. The Buddhivantha programme, however, was not evolved to measure failure or success, but to affirm growth experience.

The lack of formal structure in the non-vocational education is reflected in the places in which classes are held. In addition to classes held in proper borrowed classrooms, lessons have been given in a police station, a temple and a railway shed.

The Bosco team

The Bosco team consists of a mixture of full- and part-time paid staff and of total and partial voluntary workers. An honorary fee is paid to the five-man Salesian team. Some difficulties have been encountered in identifying and assessing the qualifications of potential staff members.

Criteria for selection

Many professionals with university degrees are looking for better-paid, less time-consuming jobs which confer greater social status. As a result, although many of the members of the team have high qualifications, it has been decided that the essential criteria for selection to the staff should be total commitment to the service of street children and a healthy, adult, altruistic personality. Any additional qualifications the newly recruited staff may have are seen as a bonus. Each new staff member serves a one-month introductory period followed by a year on probation.

Training

Personal discussion of work experience with long-established staff members has proved to be the best form of training. Tuesdays

throughout the year are devoted to training and particular attention is paid to the psychological aspects of follow-up.

In addition, staff members are given the opportunity to
attend long-duration training courses (often in Delhi) and
seminars. Quite a number of the staff have also attended more
specialized courses.

The area teams

There are ten area teams, consisting of between five and nine staff
members who provide the 'street presence' and logistics for
Bosco's ten target areas in Bangalore. The teams normally
include an area co-ordinator, a street-presence director, a street
educator, a medical auxiliary, a Buddhivantha co-ordinator and
an advocacy member. The latter is an important figure who is
instrumental in smoothing out problems of police harassment
and obtaining identity papers and licences for boys who work as
porters or hawkers.

The area teams are the linchpin of the Bosco system. They
have the heavy responsibility of making the first contact with the
street children in their 'parish', watching over their charges and
guiding them round the first obstacles of the long road to
rehabilitation and reintegration into the community. The future
of many youngsters depends on their attitude and care.

Centres of influence

The three city centres operated by Bosco – Bosco Yuvodaya,
Bosco Mane and Bosco Yuvakendra – are oases in the desert for
the street children of Bangalore.

Here, in an atmosphere of freedom and friendship, the children are helped to clear their minds of the disorder on the streets. The Bosco shelters act as a catalyst to push the children through the transition period between life on the streets and an eventual reintegration into society. They act as both day and night shelters, providing a number of facilities, including: somewhere to wash, take a bath, cook and sleep; medical aid; a place to keep their few belongings and to take advantage of savings schemes and loans; literacy classes, educational facilities and vocational training; job placement; games, picnics and audiovisual programmes; and counselling.

Plans are being drawn up for the establishment of smaller units – family-style hostels – which would be run by carefully selected house-parents. The aim would be to create as homely an atmosphere as possible. This would be the final stage in the preparation for a return to the family home. Also envisaged is a youth village, away from the city, where children could be trained for various trades and where recreational camps could be held.

These, however, are long-term plans and it will probably be a number of years before they are brought to fruition. The need for Bosco's city centres will remain and they will continue to provide a welcoming, ever-open door to Bangalore's numerous street children.

The tricks of the trade –
vocational training with Bosco

Vocational training is an important element in the Bosco curriculum even though Bosco has no purpose-built training centre of its own. A certain amount of vocational training is

Street children develop pride in belonging to a street,
to a neighbourhood, and even form affective ties with an 'ugly' environment.
Photo: © *Hien Lam-Duc*

carried out in the city centres, but most students are placed either with other institutions or with private entrepreneurs.

The decision as to which trade to follow is made on the basis of personal choice, adult counselling and the orientation programmes that precede vocational training. Staff members arrange the placement of the student and ensure that the training and other facilities, such as accommodation, are up to standard; careful follow-up is arranged to keep an eye on the student's progress.

A wide range of trades are covered. So far, students have been placed for training in the following trades: fibreglass moulding, screen printing, book-binding, carpentry, household jobs, mechanics, cover-making, tailoring, candle-making, puppetry, terracotta work, farming, computer programming, plumbing, masonry, the electrical trade and solid-waste management.

Bosco intends to establish a training centre of its own where street children will be able to be trained and a training centre outside the city where they will be able to attend short-period training camps.

A mission with a soul

The Bosco enterprise in Bangalore faces many of the same problems as similar undertakings in other big cities. Many of the remedies it is applying resemble those adopted elsewhere. Yet there can be no shadow of a doubt about it – Bosco is different. Two things stand out and really explain its success.

The first of these is the 'street presence' concept. The problem is on the streets and so are Bosco's area teams, so much so that they are a recognizable part of the streetscape like policemen, street children, buses and cars. The effect is that they are not people who have come from outside to interfere with other people's lives – they are a stable part of the everyday scene. They are 'there' and so there is no harm in talking to them.

The other factor is that, if you do talk to them, they speak the same language. This is not to say that they are all brilliant linguists who can handle any of India's many tongues and dialects – what they do is talk in terms of cultural concepts that lie deep in the heart of India's soul. *Buddhivantha* is a concept that most Indians understand. It is a clear indication that education is not just something useful, but a compelling necessity of everyday life.

As one small street child said when talking to a former director of Bosco: 'It is enough to reach *Buddhi*, we will live happily enough.'

All the world's a stage

**Paaralang Pang-tao street children project,
Manila, Philippines**

Recycling children

A dumpsite seems a curious place to set up a school, but then
everything about Paaralang Pang-tao is curious. It is a school
which has no regular funding and no teachers, only 'facilitators'.
Its students wear no uniforms and are given no grades. It started
in an empty shell of a building and much of its equipment is
made from recycled materials scavenged from the dumpsite.
Many of its students are being 'recycled' after rejection or
dropping out from the traditional school system. In other
words, Paaralang Pang-tao is in the business of recycling
children, especially children left behind by the traditional school
system.

As the school completed its fourth year of existence, nine of
its students had taken the Philippine Educational Placement
Test (PEPT) – and all nine were confident that they had passed
it successfully. Five of them were confident that they would gain
admission to high school, and the other four were still undecided
as to whether to move on to secondary education or to opt for
vocational training.

Paaralang Pang-tao is the fruit of a union between a
tightly-knit community with its own representative organization

– the Dumpsite Neighbourhood Organization (DNO) – and a group of people with humane concerns who believe that creative drama can add a new dimension to education – the Children's Laboratory for Drama in Education (Children's Lab).

With few resources between them, but a burning desire to ensure the education of their children and faith in the creativity innate in all human beings, these two organizations have created a growing and successful school adapted to the specific needs of the children in the area.

These needs include flexible school hours which enable the children to continue to work and contribute to the family income and the constant reinvention of the children's creativity, self-esteem and sense of identity.

The philosophy of Paaralang Pang-tao encourages students to see themselves as active participants in the learning process, not merely passive recipients of knowledge.

During the first phase of Paaralang Pang-tao, shortage of funds drew out the resourcefulness of all those in the project and acted as a spur to creativity. But as the project grows in complexity funding will have to be placed on a firmer basis.

Harsh economic realities make it increasingly difficult to rely too heavily on voluntary effort and all the personal sacrifice that this involves. The question has been raised of calling for financial support from some of the comparatively well-off Western arts councils.

Some people may also question whether a pedagogical system based on Drama in Education can be generalized and implemented by people without basic theatrical experience.

These reservations in no way diminish the very clear message that emerges from the Paaralang Pang-tao project and from which other community-based projects for street children could benefit.

Paaralang Pang-tao's message is clear:

- Get the community behind you and you will find that you have tapped into an immense fund of creativity and resource-fulness.
- Accept the child as an individual, creative person at the centre of everything you undertake.
- Give the child room to breathe. Forget about teaching in the traditional sense and look at education as a shared learning and creative experience.

The philosophy of Paaralang Pang-tao encourages students to see themselves as active participants in the learning process, not merely passive recipients of knowledge.

Located in the community of Baranggay Payatas, about 8 km from Quezon City, Paaralang Pang-tao (The Humane School) is indeed a most unusual establishment. It is situated on the edge of a garbage dumpsite and is run jointly by the Children's Lab and DNO.

The population of Payatas is estimated at 10,000, most of whom work as labourers or survive by scavenging on the dumpsite. They live in houses built of a mixture of concrete and plywood. The roofs are made of iron sheeting, anchored down against the wind by the weight of hollow concrete blocks and old car tyres.

The school stands on a 300 m^2 site acquired by DNO in 1985. The children and their parents live in the area surrounding the dumpsite and work as scavengers. When the decision was made to create a school adapted to the special needs of the dumpsite children, finding and selecting candidates was no problem at all.

The need for education is strongly felt by DNO members.

The single formal school in the area can accommodate only a small number of children and it has a high drop-out rate, in keeping with the national average.

When the announcement of the opening of an alternative school was made, over 100 children wanted to enlist. Since the resources available at that time were limited, priority was given to the children of DNO members.

Enrolment requirements

The only requirements for enrolment are a willingness and desire to learn; even those who consider themselves 'too old to come to school' are welcome. Given that DNO members' children get priority, preference goes to children: (a) who participated in the Theatre Group organized in 1989; (b) who have dropped out of school; (c) who have, for one reason or another, been refused admission to the local elementary school; (d) whose parents (mostly DNO members) have decided that there is really no point in their children attending formal school; and (e) whose families were displaced by armed conflict in the rural areas and were obliged to migrate and settle next to the dumpsite.

The school building

The school is designed to have a homelike rather than an institutional atmosphere. The facilities found in the average home are more in evidence than the blackboards and desks of a traditional classroom. This, in turn, encourages the children to form quasi-family groupings in which tasks and responsibilities are assigned according to the abilities of each individual group member.

While every effort is being made to improve the learning environment by making ample space and materials available, care has to be taken not to overwhelm the children by providing over-sophisticated facilities which, experience shows, can make the children feel uneasy and alienated. Much of the equipment is made by parents from materials acquired or recycled from the dumpsite. Only items that are absolutely essential are purchased.

An unusual partnership

Paaralang Pang-tao is the fruit of an unusual partnership.

DNO is a registered people's organization, set up to defend the interests of people living in 'Smoky Valley', as the dumpsite area has come to be known. The need for such an organization becomes clearer when it is realized that there are no transport or postal services in the area and that the dumpsite itself does not even figure on any official city map.

The Children's Lab is a cultural organization promoting the use of drama in education as a learning and teaching method. It evolved out of a troupe known as the Textbook Theatre (1982) which elaborated understandable performance modules in science, mathematics and communication arts as a supplement to elementary education.

It was found that these modules were equally effective tools when performed by children, so Theatre by Children (1986) was created, for performances in public parks and squares. This was followed by the founding of Voice (1989) which takes as its themes the wider issues affecting the lives of street children.

These all represent the street-based activities now brought together under the Children's Lab programme. Paaralang Pang-tao officially opened its doors for the school year 1989/90 and was the first community-based venture undertaken by the Children's Lab.

Funding

The resources of both DNO and the Children's Lab are mobilized to fund the Paaralang Pang-tao project. The Children's Lab provides the Drama in Education and Children's Theatre (DIECT) teachers – or 'facilitators' as they prefer to be called – and each year trains three DNO volunteers on the job.

Funds for the construction and maintenance of the building as well as materials and supplies used for the project come from individual, voluntary contributions and from organizations such as the Urban Basic Services Programme of Quezon City. This was how the installation of a concrete floor was funded in 1990.

In 1991, a fund-raising campaign, based mainly on the sale of old newspapers and other recyclable junk from the dumpsite, produced the money to buy the necessary school supplies and textbooks for the school year. In the same year, voluntary contributions from parents covered the cost of the meagre allowance paid to volunteer-trainees. More recently, when the night-school programme was due to begin, a foreign volunteer's family donated 5,000 pesos (about $200) for the installation of electricity. Other needs (first-aid kits, tables, chairs, blackboards) are funded from the Children's Lab's other sources – mostly from personal friends and funds earned through its training programme.

It takes considerable faith and courage to operate on this kind of shoe-string funding. Very few organizations would have had the courage to open a school in a shell of a building with an earth floor. In spite of this, the project went ahead and in three short years the tumble-down shell had been transformed into an effective, fully functioning, comparatively well-equipped school. This had been possible because, from the outset, Paaralang Pang-tao was seen as the community's own school.

One of the major achievements of the project has been to motivate parents and obtain their full backing. This has been done through close collaboration with DNO and by such measures as issuing a dossier to parents every year to explain the aims and workings of the school. Through DNO, parents are heavily involved and are prepared to make donations and organize fund-raising campaigns for *their* school. Some have trained as facilitators and some of the younger ones attend the night school.

No major funding organizations have offered to help with the project. There is a feeling that they are not yet ready to fund the alternative teaching the project offers until results are obvious or until conditions have changed so much that they run counter to the very targets set by DNO.

A Western account would, undoubtedly, express horror at Paaralang Pang-tao's 'need-based' acquisition of material, financial and human resources, but it teaches everyone creativity and resourcefulness. Paaralang Pang-tao is truly the product of a collective effort.

The facilitators

At Paaralang Pang-tao there are no teachers, only 'facilitators'. This is no empty play on words, but a constant reminder of the philosophy that underlies the project. Whereas the traditional role of the teacher is to expound and that of the pupil to absorb what is expounded, the facilitator is a person who, as the word implies, makes it easier for the students to learn for themselves. At Paaralang Pang-tao, the facilitators see themselves as learners too.

They are not figures to be afraid of, but friends who respond when addressed as 'Uncle', 'Aunt' or even 'Elder Brother' or 'Elder Sister'. A facilitator will even comfort a child, and clean and bandage any minor cuts or wounds, whether inside or outside the classroom.

At present, the staff consists of a project manager/trainer, a finance officer/street educator, a project co-ordinator and a volunteer facilitator, all from the Children's Lab, and three volunteer facilitators, all trained by the Children's Lab, from DNO. There are also normally three trainee volunteer facilitators undergoing a year's on-the-job training.

From the start, facilitators are made aware that their purpose is not to 'domesticate' the children but to liberate them. The children are not the problem – they are a manifestation of a wider problem of social injustice. The aim is to allow learners to take responsibility for their own learning and achievement and to give them control of their education rather than treating them as passive participants.

Training of facilitators

In addition to on-the-job training, trainee facilitators attend a series of workshops and seminars conducted by the Children's Lab. They also attend workshops and training sessions prepared by other organizations. During the time that they are in training the volunteers are officially referred to as *kapwa,* or fellow learners.

The two main pillars of the training schedule are: the two-day

Basic Orientation Workshop covering analysis of both the national and local situations and the need for alternative education
which begins every volunteer facilitator's training and the Basic
Drama in Education and Children's Theatre Workshop whose
purpose is to raise the trainee's levels of consciousness, self-aware-
ness and creativity. This workshop includes a preliminary contact
with the methodology of play and game. Curriculum-building,
lesson-planning and the preparation of materials are the subject of
the workshop/seminar on alternative education practices and
techniques.

Altogether the volunteer facilitators' training takes the
equivalent of a month and a half. The training sessions are
staggered and are flexible enough to fit in with the volunteers'
extremely tight schedule in the community. Most of those who
sign on for training are mothers and young people who have just
completed secondary school but who, for economic reasons, do
not intend to go on to college.

Over the last three school years, the Children's Lab has trained
ten volunteers, three of whom remain active in the programme.
The rest have joined other community programmes, often health
programmes, run by other organizations. The main reason for this
is economic. All that the project can afford in the way of a mon-
etary allowance for the volunteers is 100 pesos ($4) a week and
even this is proving a struggle to maintain. Those who volunteer
as health workers not only receive a better allowance, but also
receive benefits in kind, such as medicines and food rations.

Unfortunately, Paaralang Pang-tao has no such advantages
to offer. Even the permanent Children's Lab staff receive very
low salaries, dependent upon the income from training
programmes and other Children's Lab projects. As things stand
at the moment, Paaralang Pang-tao has to try to keep three

volunteers for a year while training three more to take their place the following year. Volunteers who leave the programme usually excel in their work with other organizations.

The traditional methods of teaching are not wrong, but they are incomplete. They fail to give emphasis to the activities of social interaction and communication.

The curriculum

Contrary to the custom in most formal schools, at Paaralang Pang-tao children are grouped by age rather than by grade. This enables them to go through the process of socialization with children of their own age but, at the same time, to tackle their school assignments at their own pace and according to their capabilities.

Since the methodology of drama in education is the core pedagogy on which the programme is based, the children are given the opportunity to experience the different aspects of theatre. The key starting points in the three main curriculum sectors are drawn from these theatrical experiences.

The Parent's Dossier, which is given to all parents at the beginning of the school year, describes the curriculum in terms of these age levels.

The play group and pre-school levels (age 2 to 6)

In the play group (age 2 to 3) the children play and learn to be with other children and to socialize. They learn about cleanliness, acquire values and learn to look after their own belongings; in short, they learn to live in a community.

Agricultural activities play an important part in non-formal education.
This young girl is trying to distinguish between different types of cereals.
Photo: © UNICEF

In the pre-school levels (age 3 to 6) the children are prepared to face academic challenges and to acquire basic skills such as reading, writing and mathematics.

Both the play group and the pre-school levels enjoy story-telling sessions, simple discovery experiments, and performing and fine arts.

Levels 1 and 2 (age 7 to 9)

Most of the children assigned to these levels are children who were enrolled in a traditional school but dropped out or, when pre-tested, were found lacking in reading, writing and comprehension skills in Tagalog. They are therefore introduced to alternative learning methods.

Mathematics and its applications are reinforced at these levels. The children are introduced to more complicated assignments and are encouraged to move on to acquiring reading and writing skills in English.

Levels 3 and 4 (age 10 to 11)

The children are now considered to be ready to achieve a degree of competency in the second language (English) and this is the primary objective at these levels. It is not enough for the children to be able to read and write the assignments given them; they must also fully understand them. This is because the science and mathematics tasks are mostly written in English. Once they have achieved the zero mistake objective in their assignments, the children are expected to move smoothly and rapidly on to using work-books and drills, and to completing their assignments at these levels.

Levels 5 and 6 (age 12 to 13)

The children are assumed to be ready to take the PEPT. They are expected to have achieved an acceptable level in communication arts, social and natural sciences and mathematics. Children who decide to continue their secondary education (high school) are encouraged to take PEPT. If they decide not to continue, these levels provide the opportunity for children to survey the other options open to them.

If children see themselves learning a trade such as carpentry, for example, or running a small business instead of continuing schooling, the school facilitators will provide them with the necessary reading materials and contacts for them to pursue this aim.

The objective is to show the children that there are many choices open to them other than high school or college, and that one can become a fine carpenter or a good entrepreneur with no loss of self-esteem.

Youth and adult levels (14 and over)

The young people (14 to 21) and adults (22 and over) in these levels may not have had the opportunity to finish elementary or high school, or may have been to high school and dropped out. These levels provide a chance to rediscover their skills and strengths, their shortcomings and weaknesses. The programme provides remedial classes and revision to make up for perceived shortcomings and weaknesses. These may range from poor reading ability to comprehension failure or simply loss of self-esteem. Again the options are open to take PEPT and, for the younger ones, to enter the mainstream school system, or to go for vocational training.

Paaralang Pang-tao does not nurture the illusion that all the children enrolled are bound for higher academic education or will complete a university course. This would be neither honest nor realistic. Instead Paaralang Pang-tao teaches its children that it is their right to be educated and that, as young people, they have to begin to exercise this right and make the effort to participate in matters concerning them, their homes, the community and the nation.

Part Four

The all-important administration

Street and working children, by nature, call into question the very values of society. Administering and organizing their rehabilitation requires skill and understanding of their specific characteristics. There is no single way in which a school or centre for street children can be run and, as is stressed in many of the projects, each child is a special case.

Street and working children particularly need to know they are being helped. They need reassuring that they are in good hands and that those taking care of them are efficient and responsible. This authority is more symbolic than real as each child demands a true sense of affection. The child, therefore, has to be in constant contact with the educators and even participate in his or her own reorganization and integration into society. This means joining in discussions on planning or helping educators find points of interest.

The actual structure of the centres is all-important. Some organizations take the children in, others prefer to place the children in guardian families. Many of the children have lacked the most basic family role and need reassurance in their identity and behaviour. The JUCONI project in Mexico asks any existing family member to be involved in the process of integration as contact with family or friends is vital. In the Home of Love (Madras), instructors avoid pushing the children for immediate results, as this frightens them away. Results are secondary and only important at the time of reintroduction into any formal kind of schooling. This idea of the collective spirit appeared in both the Peruvian and the Colombian projects described earlier. The children come together, share and, in so doing, achieve. In the Hogares Don Bosco in Argentina, the children are placed within small groups in independent hostels. They are psychologically prepared for each new move up the scale of hostels and, at each new stage, a greater self-reliance is acquired. All centres are obviously structured around the children yet the children must feel they are in charge of their own lives. The arguments for and against night or day shelters are numerous as are the pros and cons of restricting the children's freedom. Results, like methods, vary, but the centres know that if one child can be saved then all efforts have been worth while.

The pibes *of the* '*little hearths*'

Hogares Don Bosco project,
Buenos Aires, Argentina

The children in this project live in the streets of the outer suburbs of Buenos Aires, a huge expanse of territory housing 7 million people, or close to a quarter of the country's population.

As in so many countries, the outskirts of the city are full of families from the unskilled labour-force, recently uprooted from the rural world. They have failed to find a stable job and live a hand-to-mouth existence on the fringes of the big city, in a chronic state of underemployment or outright unemployment. In many cases, poor cultural adaptation to new conditions, housing problems, a father's unemployment and low wages gradually spawn alcoholism, delinquency, ill-treatment and family break-ups. Street children, that is, both children 'of' the street, and children 'in' the street, are the result of such a mix of cultural, economic and social problems.

Children 'in' the street are those who, by day, sell trinkets, sweets or small pictures for a few coins, but who go back to their homes and families at night. It is the tremendous poverty or disunity of such families which drives children into the streets. There is certainly considerable preventive work to be done, at such a stage, if a permanent break with the family unit is to be avoided.

However, it is mostly the children 'of' the street, strictly speaking, that the Argentine project is aimed at. These children, fleeing from hunger or the indifference of their family environment, form groups known as *ranchadas* who prowl around railway stations, bus stops and city squares. They have developed a true subculture, with its own behaviour patterns, values, specific attitudes and language. Their activities reflect this subculture. They resort to drugs to forget the hunger, cold and other problems. They get money by opening taxi doors in the hope of small tips; they also get money through prostitution and theft. Paradoxically enough, these children reproduce, within their own groups, the very hierarchical model they originally ran away from. They are extremely aggressive and wary, and are united only when confronting the outside world.

Leaving aside their social context, one might only see these young people as children with psychological problems where certain negative patterns of behaviour could be modified. If their social environment is taken into account, however, then it is obvious that such behaviour patterns, or character traits, are vital to anyone trying to live or survive in the street world. This environment has actually spurred these children to develop a whole series of qualities which one ought to try to put to good use, qualities such as intuition, practical intelligence, sharp-wittedness, boldness, capacity for organization and imagination. The Hogares Don Bosco project's starting-point is recognizing this duality and contradictory reality within these children's personalities.

It is well known that the common ideal of brotherhood and justice behind the activities of all groups struggling to help street children includes very diverse social, political and religious orientations. In Argentina, as elsewhere, the Don Bosco Hostels, created by the Salesian Order, reflect a dual objective, one that is both social and religious: to bring up good citizens and to educate good Christians. The Order's activities, nevertheless, include forms of instruction that benefit everyone, regardless of any specific religious affiliation. This is because the attainment of their first aim requires passing through secondary stages. These stages are multiple and common to most organizations helping children: creating an environment where the child can learn the meaning of hope; offering the youth educational prospects; ultimately reintegrating the child into society; and bringing the young person up as full adult.

On 18 May 1985, after three months of preparation, the first *hogar* or hostel was opened in La Boca, one of the poorest districts of Buenos Aires. This was the San Pedro hostel and the first child taken in was a typical example of a street child: Ricardo Luján, aged 13, had been sleeping for the previous four months in a railway station. The second hostel, the San Jorge, opened in the same district in November 1986. Six children are living there today and a move to new premises where fifteen children could be accommodated, is being considered. The first hostel has already moved and was renamed the San Juan Bosco hostel in April 1987. It has been specifically designed to deal with children 'in' the street, that is, those from destitute families where husband and wife are in constant opposition. Fourteen children are now sheltered there, including several brothers.

In November 1988, a day centre, the Miguel Magone, opened near the railway terminus. Street educators working on the project try to make contact, at night, with those children who have just arrived in town. They usually come from the suburbs and roam around near the station. The educators try to bring them to the day centre, where sixty or so children spend some time between 9 a.m. and 6 p.m. A dozen children sleep there, temporarily, while waiting to be transferred to other hostels.

Finally, in March 1989, a boarding house, the Independencia, was created for 'ex-street children'. These are young people, now at work, who can meet their own expenses partially. There are seven of these youngsters, now well on their way to becoming permanently self-reliant. The Casita hostel, which opened in August 1990, houses six youths (aged 14 to 17) in the western part of the city. Two more hostels have been opened, one in September 1992 and another in April 1993. They can house, respectively, six to ten children.

The method

The approach here is step-by-step because there is a clear awareness that success can never be obtained immediately. First these children must be contacted wherever they are actually found. Then the street educator may, perhaps, persuade them to go to the day centre where patient attempts are made to wean the child off certain habits. The third step is entry into the 'little hostels'. These hostels are purposefully small. The aim is to re-create, at least in part, a family atmosphere where activities can be carried out together – work, study, house chores, sports and other forms of recreation. They are 'open house' hostels and all lengthy searches for the youngsters' families start here. For some youngsters, a last, optional step is available. This is the boarding house, where the sufficiently mature can live while meeting some of the expenses themselves. The project continues to offer them support and lodging until they feel that they can live completely independently.

Drugs help children to fight suffering,
but also endanger their mental and physical health.
Photo: *Hien Lam-Duc*

A process of constant reassessment

The project is subject to a process of constant reassessment and review. Each week, in each hostel, meetings are held in which both children and counsellors take part.

The project's staff also hold a meeting. Every fortnight, a Hostels Council meets, attended by representatives from all the hostels. This council is responsible for assessing, correcting and setting the future course of the project, suggesting standards and means for the preparation of the educational project and preparing the general assemblies. These are held at least twice a year. All those responsible for the project, as well as all the project's beneficiaries, participate.

All the same, it is the Salesian Order which has the last word on educational and administrative aspects of projects. The Order is also responsible for staff salaries, maintenance of the hostels and expenses for food, clothes and health care for the children. Further resources are obtained by different means, for example through sponsorship by public bodies, voluntary contributions from different centres of the Salesian Order and aid campaigns (for food and medicines) organized by parishes or family organizations.

How many children are there?

In the first phase, that is at street level, the number of children concerned varies considerably. Educators mingle with groups of up to eight or ten children (generally boys), aged between 8 and 18. Their numbers vary in the day centres, although it is safe to say that, on a daily basis, there is an average of about

fifty children and adolescents. In the 'little hostels', the numbers are calculated with care and there are between six and
eight youngsters in each (there are now seven hostels). A selection process exists and the initiative comes from the street educator because he or she is the one who first makes contact with
the children. Thereafter the children have to give their own reasons for wanting to stay on and progress through the various
phases.

From street to hostel

In the street, educators usually make contact with the children
between 11 p.m. and 2 a.m. The aim is not only to meet children
but also to learn about their environment. A good knowledge of
group dynamics makes it possible to choose the most effective
way of initiating contact in the streets or city squares, either by
striking up a song or by playing the guitar. Some educators hand
round some maté to sip, or play some game or other (especially
soccer). When a relationship of trust has been forged, the child
can then be made to understand that another way of life is indeed
possible.

First the child should be made to know that there is a place
where he or she can find a roof, some food and a little affection – the day centre. The child is generally introduced to this
place by the street educator, although there is some flexibility
in the various conditions laid down by each centre. The
street educator takes charge of his or her ward from this stage
onwards. In the day centre, the child will find initial solutions to
the most pressing problems – food, hygiene and health –
then basic information on drugs, AIDS and alcoholism.

Educational guidance and, if necessary, literacy instruction are available. In addition there are sports, and in certain cases, preliminary job guidance. Finally, and most importantly, the centre offers the child an environment where certain very basic norms can be appreciated: no theft, no drugs, no violence. Every week, in one of the scheduled meetings, the child will have a chance to express feelings, to take stock of the situation and observe other boarders, and to try to assess the climate of advance.

The crucial decision occurs when the youth moves from the day centre to the little hostel. This truly is a decision. The child must be absolutely certain that he or she wants to go to the hostel and make this request known firmly and explicitly. Luckily, the youngster already knows some of the children in the hostel and a constant dialogue between the teams in the day centres and those in the hostels maintains ties. Then there is a transition phase when the child, who has expressed the wish, prepares both practically and emotionally for the transfer to the hostel. Practically speaking, the child must be capable of living up to any commitment and must have already fully accepted a number of those standards basic to communal life. In this way, the youth can, immediately and profitably, share in all the activities at the hostel. The importance of this passage should not be underestimated.

The 'little hostel' sets out, above all, to be a home, that is to say, somewhere fixed and stable, where the child can weave ties devoid of aggression and steeped in mutual respect and kindness. The child must also learn self-respect and for this to occur, all youngsters must know how to take each other's specific life story into proper account. Every one of these youngsters' life-stories is unique and this is one of the reasons for the choice of 'little hostels' so that the child can have the opportunity of getting to know and understand his or her fellows.

Each 'little hostel' is also a place where every child learns to give practical meaning to such words as 'education', 'work' and 'health' through participation in activities. Each and every activity in the hostel can be made to yield 'educational' benefit, but there are no specifically educational activities at these hostels. Children at the same hostel may actually go to different schools. There is no one school for street children, nor do the organizers of the project believe one to be desirable. All the same, the hostels' form of educational activity does require the project's educators to have specific training and the children receiving formal education must be closely monitored, psychologically, educationally and medically, by the project's professional staff.

It is also necessary to instil a work ethic at the earliest stage possible. Children and especially adolescents must be taught to see the link between sustained regular effort and equally regular income. Recognizing the importance of one's own health is no less vital. Strict health checks are periodically carried out, and continuous information is given – formally and informally – on all health problems of possible importance to street children.

It should, however, be pointed out that there are, at present, no 'hostels' specifically geared to deal with those children who are too seriously disturbed psychologically or who suffer from very serious physical or mental handicaps. In the same way, although by no means a formal rule, an attempt is made not to take all children deeply involved in alcoholism or drug addiction. This is a limitation, but also a choice because it prevents 'ordinary' activities at the hostels from stopping before an appropriate solution to problems like drug abuse can be found.

Other more immediately material aspects, such as food and clothing, receive equally important consideration. The children's specific needs, according to age, are carefully watched by a dietician, and the latter plans each fortnight's menus. Appropriate diets are prescribed for those children suffering from specific deficiencies, which is unhappily not a rare occurrence.

There is also an educational aspect to the way the children relate to their clothing, and this should by no means be overlooked. The children are not used to taking care of their clothes. They do not understand what it means to wash them, or even to buy them. It is important to make them understand that what they wear forms such an essential element of their appearance and is not something to be worn threadbare and then thrown away after something new has been stolen.

A child's need for protection, whether from a legal or a social point of view, is something quite different, of course, but it is an essential need which must also be met. The children not only lack protectors but often enough they do not even have any identification papers. Children in the hostels are placed under the authority of a magistrate, that is, they come under a precise legal framework. In addition, the educators, as well as the various lawyers connected with the project, are responsible for dealing with the many problems with the police or legal authorities. Most of the youngsters were initially in situations that were irregular by definition. The street educator himself, who often works late at night and in social environments under the eye of the police, in turn requires his own legal justifications and legal safeguards.

The characteristics of an educator

To choose to work with street children is to choose a particular way of life. Street children are youngsters who live in abnormal or exceptional circumstances. Street educators and other 'street professionals' must, in turn, learn to live and take action in such exceptional circumstances. A street educator's work is professional work, no doubt, but one for which university degrees are not enough. Academic knowledge must be constantly improved by continual self-training and personal research.

In the educator's eyes, every child, by definition, is 'recoverable'. The educator is not just interested in the sort of 'assistance' which skirts round more deep-seated problems. He aims for the individual's all-round, integrated training. The qualities required of an educator are thus numerous, and it is sometimes difficult to find them all in a single person. Motivation is needed, as well as ability to understand and analyse one's own motivations. The educator must also be able to forge ties with people for whom suspicion has become a rule of life and be familiar in far more than 'academic' terms with the reality at hand. He or she must also have a thorough knowledge of group dynamics and be able to work in a team. More important still is considerable psychological and emotional stability for, whether in the street, centre, or hostel, the educator remains the child's model, and that is a tremendous responsibility.

It is equally important for the educator to be young. Relations based on friendship, verging indeed nearly on brotherhood, are easier to forge where there is no great difference in age. The average age for an educator in the project ranges between 22 and 32. There are, of course, a few maturer individuals, aged 35 to 55, who play a more parental role. In each hostel, there is also a woman, aged between 40 and 50, who shoulders a number of domestic tasks and offers the children an equally vital maternal image.

All in all, the project has around thirty educators and a team of professionals which includes three psychologists, two educational psychology specialists, three social workers, two lawyers, five administrators with a variety of tasks and three people responsible for the general co-ordination of the project.

The chiquillos
of Puebla

The JUCONI Foundation project, Puebla, Mexico

The need for education can sometimes be so pressing that one can forget that the educational process can also be enriching for the educator. The project of the Fundación Junto con los Niños de Puebla (JUCONI) demonstrates that there may be many delays and diversions before the right formula is discovered.

The origin of the project is to be found in a study carried out in 1987 by five organizations (governmental, non-governmental and religious) on the situation of the street children of Puebla. Two separate projects arose from the study. The first, a governmental project, evolved into a prevention programme which, in practical terms, ceased to exist after 1991. The second project, taken over by a British organization, the International Children's Trust, at the instigation of two Mexican organizations (the Fundación Fuad Abed Halabi and the Instituto Poblano de Readaptación), developed into the JUCONI programme. JUCONI was started in 1989 by a group of nine people (seven Mexicans and two British nationals). Their aim was 'to offer young people working or living in the streets, or who run a significant risk of doing either, the possibility of improving their living conditions'. JUCONI receives financial aid from the International Children's Trust and, in 1993,

UNESCO contributed substantially to the financing of its educational programme.

Getting the balance right

JUCONI has tried to distinguish very clearly between its 'administrative' and its 'operational' activities, between the project management structures and everything connected with social and educational matters. A study of organizations in Mexico with similar aims shows that they all too often fall into one of two traps: either they develop a top-heavy bureaucratic-administrative system which stifles the operational section, or else they find themselves in a chaotic administrative void, which allows charismatic leaders to overwhelm the project with their personal obsessions. Activities then become centred around an individual and not a programme.

It was therefore necessary to set up a solid but scrupulously open form of administration that could adapt to the needs and demands of the operational section. This was not an easy task, and the time and effort invested (more than two years) may seem excessive to some. Yet experience has shown that, in the long run, meticulous preparation in this domain is rewarding at all levels. A clearly defined legal status, strictly kept accounts, a rational work pattern and real discipline are all valued by educators who may have experienced situations in which sentimentality or a vague religiosity predominated or in which the organization was overpowered by the weight of certain personalities.

The first steps

Field work had started in the spring of 1988, before the actual creation of JUCONI, when a few young educators decided to start a voluntary assistance service. This was made up of recreational activities and set up in eight locations in the city for the benefit of working children. By the end of 1988 some thirty children were participating regularly in the activities of Operación Amistad. In 1989, these young educators were incorporated into the framework of the JUCONI project, which then consisted of five main elements: the Administrative Department, the Operational Department, Operación Amistad, a day centre and a transition home.

After two years' operation (1989–90), the project had achieved several tangible results. As a result of Operación Amistad, that is, of direct operation on the streets, 130 working or street children were able to benefit from the project in its first year and in the second year this figure rose to 142. The transition home accommodated thirty-four street children in 1989 and thirty-three in 1990. As for the day centre, some fifty children stayed there each year for periods of varying duration. During this first phase, however, the project encountered problems and discovered answers of benefit to anyone involved in street projects.

The main lesson to be learned from this first phase is that working children and street children present separate social and psychological realities. Their needs are not the same and their problems require specific treatment. It is even desirable that the educators themselves should specialize in dealing with only one of the two categories. It is also preferable to arrange for the physical separation of the two groups (premises, activities, etc.), which was not done during the first phase of JUCONI.

Continuity is equally essential. For example, in the early days, many children were admitted directly to the transition home without being prepared beforehand within the framework of Operación Amistad; as a result, the educators' task was made considerably more complicated.

The present situation

The review of the first two years led to two important changes. First, Operación Amistad was reshaped (specific teams of educators were created for each group of children) and the structure of the project was simplified (the services of the day centre were restricted to working children). The project was divided into two sub-programmes. Help for Working Children now consists of three services: Operación Amistad, the day centre and 'popular education' (see below). Help for Street Children provides two services: Operación Amistad (street section) and the transition home.

The second innovation was the creation of a Popular Education service. In certain areas of the town, the educators talked to the families where the children were in high-risk situations in an attempt to treat the problem at source through discussions, the organization of workshops, and educating and raising awareness before the children became street workers or street children.

Help for working children

Children working in the street or those in high-risk situations covered by the project (100 in 1992–93) range in age from 3 to 17 and are mostly male (75 per cent). They have generally been to primary school and are not strictly speaking illiterate; nevertheless, they all have serious difficulty in reading, writing and even oral expression (Spanish is often not their mother-tongue). Some 77 per cent of them are of rural origin and most live in homes where the mother assumes the major responsibility for parental care and control, either because the father is absent or because he is indifferent to the children's lot. Such families live in conditions of extreme poverty.

The objectives of the programme for street and working children are realistic. Where this is financially possible for the family, the aim is to encourage the child to return to school on a full-time basis and abandon all work in the street or, at least, only work there part-time. In most cases, the most important task is to protect the children from exploitation, abuse and ill-treatment. The children and their families must be made aware of the dangers they are facing and of the practical possibilities of improving their working conditions.

As a first step, the field-worker educators of Operación Amistad set up clubs for young street workers. At the first club meeting with the few children with whom he or she has managed to establish a relationship of trust, the educator will suggest they bring other children they know to the next meeting. The new club will have four to twelve members who have certain affinities and common characteristics (age, employer, origin, etc.). After a few meetings the children will choose a leader from amongst themselves. He or she will see to the organization of subsequent meetings and establish a permanent connection between the children and the educator. Each club has its own programme of activities, essentially sport and recreational activities.

Education must reach out and speak to children in their own terms,
adapt to their personality and take their specific experiences into account.
Photo: © *UNICEF/Francene Keery*

After the first few months, the more motivated children are invited to participate regularly in the activities of the day centre. There, they follow a year-long programme of elementary education and have the use of various services (canteen or food aid, showers, dispensary, etc.). At the day centre the children are organized in age-groups (8 to 10, 11 to 13 and 14 to 17), each consisting of a dozen children. Twice a week, the children attend programme meetings. Each meeting lasts two hours or so. It is divided into three sections:

- A practical part during which the children learn several basic elements of everyday life (personal hygiene, nutrition, cleaning, health-care).
- A year-long training programme which focuses on a different theme each term (such as 'The Individual and his/her Surroundings', 'Communication', 'Work', and 'Prospects'). This is a general training programme which attempts to make the children more open to the world around them. It also aims to motivate the children and direct them towards work or leisure activities that are far removed from the street.
- Lastly, they are taught leisure and manual activities that are connected with the themes studied. Sport is also practised.

One of the most original aspects of the programme is a section of the Popular Education project where, alongside work with the children, systematic action is aimed at the parents (the mothers essentially). The principal method adopted is the organization of workshops, generally at the home of one of the mothers, so the participants can acquire the basics of needlework, weaving, cooking, etc. Slowly, the groups evolve into conversation groups in which the women learn to discuss their problems among themselves and work out their own solutions.

Help for street children

In 1992–93, 110 street children participated in the different phases of the project. The average age of this almost exclusively male population (98 per cent boys) ranged from 11 to 17. The level of education of these children is not significantly different from that of the working children. The proportion of children of urban origin is greater (44 per cent, as opposed to 56 per cent of rural origin). Family difficulties are more or less the same, differing only in degree.

During the initial phase, there is a fundamental difference between the method used to approach street children and the one used to contact working children. Experience has shown that it is of little use to form groups. What counts is establishing individual contact with each child. Relationships are established primarily in the streets but the educators also visit centres for supervised education where they try to single out children with ability, motivation and particular interests.

At this stage, the educators provide the children with various recreational activities and food aid. This phase can last from a few weeks to a few months (six months maximum). Then, the educators select the children who seem most able to adjust successfully to the new lifestyle which will be theirs in the transition or JUCONI home.

According to the organizers, experience has shown that it serves no useful purpose to provide a day centre for the children during the phase of first contact. Paradoxically, this safe place where the children can enjoy the basic comforts, even if only temporarily, tends, in reality, to prolong the stay of certain children on the street by making life there more bearable.

The selected child becomes a 'candidate'. The educators create a file and his or her case is analysed thoroughly. Contacts with the child intensify and, after about a month, he or she is admitted to the JUCONI home. The minimum duration of the stay is three months (the maximum being eighteen months). Preferably no more than twenty children or adolescents are accommodated at any one time. The group thus created follows an annual programme which is divided into four terms. The programme includes schooling to bring the child up to the level of education corresponding to his or her age, group or individual psychotherapy, leisure activities, and care and maintenance of the home. Going out, sport and contacts with the outside world all are restricted to weekends.

A 'life project' for the term is devised for each child when he or she moves into the house. It is composed of nine objectives that are common to all children and one objective that is specific to each individual case. On the basis of these nine objectives, a weekly evaluation of the children's results is made. The organizers have noticed that one of the children's biggest problems is their inability to express their thoughts and feelings satisfactorily. Hence, great importance is given to written, oral and body language.

Every evening, the children take part in a communication workshop designed to promote progress in this field. The techniques they learn must enable them, in particular, to express what the educators call 'family anguish' and to try to re-establish contact with their families by reducing this very feeling of anguish. This will, it is hoped, lead to a degree of emotional stability.

Prospects

For the working children, the ultimate objective is to keep them in, or re-introduce them to, the formal education system on a full-time basis. This enables them to reinforce their identities as children and strengthen their family ties. Ideally, they would stop working or at least stop working in the street. Fulfilment of this objective, however, comes up against the basic facts of the economic and social situation in Mexico. According to certain sources, over 45 per cent of the active population participates in the so-called informal economy. This is the case, in particular, of most of the families concerned. It is therefore necessary to persuade the parents that, even though it might be an economic necessity for the children to work, this must not be an exclusive activity and that the children's future must be preserved by keeping them in school, even if only part-time.

What results has the JUCONI programme achieved with regard to these two groups of children? On the basis of the information available to them, the organizers were able to establish that in 1991–92 only 30 per cent of the children and teenagers who participated in the project completely left the street. All the working children frequenting the day centre were attending school and their academic performance had improved substantially. As for the 'at-risk' children from families concerned by the activities of the Popular Education sub-programme, they were all attending school, either in the formal system or at a centre for specialized education.

For the street children who were accommodated at the JUCONI home, the aim was either to achieve their return to their families or, if that was not possible, their placement with a specialized institution or even to enable them to lead an independent life if they were old enough. This aim was achieved in 60 per cent of cases. A programme to monitor the subsequent evolution of these children is being set up.

The aims and results of the programme must not be judged

or assessed from the perspective of the general problem of street children around Puebla. Clearly, the scale of this social problem is such that it would be absurd to expect solutions from a single organization were it a hundred times wealthier than JUCONI. Within the limits of its own resources, the JUCONI programme tries to provide concrete help so as to improve the living conditions of these children and allow them the opportunity of benefiting from a normal education. Although the programme concerns only a small number of children and adolescents, if it enables them to affirm their identities, take initiatives, improve their communication skills and strengthen their will to fight for better living conditions, it will have achieved its aims.

Homes of love

Don Bosco Anbu Illam Society (DBAI), Madras, India

The context

The Don Bosco Anbu Illam Society (DBAI) is a group of bodies
or shelters spread all over Madras and managed by a charitable
agency to rehabilitate children at risk, especially street children,
girls or boys, aged between 10 and 18. There are sixteen centres
known as Homes of Love (Don Bosco Anbu Illam). DBAI is
established in the heart of the city of Madras, capital of the state
of Tamil Nadu in southern India. Madras, founded by the
(English) East India Company in 1639 on the coast of the Bay of
Bengal, is the oldest Western-style city in India and is today the
fourth largest urban area in the country. It spreads over 600 km^2
and has a population of 5 million (1987). Although the city is a
port and very busy, there are 1 million economically weak
persons, 56 per cent of whom have no vocational qualifications.
Over 800,000 poor families eke out a living there, 171,000 of
them in slums. From these disadvantaged families come
35,000 children who survive in an urban social fabric which
appears to ignore them and no longer inspires in them either
trust or hope.

Who are the street children?

Of the 35,000 street children in Madras, 87.2 per cent are homeless. DBAI divides these children up into a dozen groups identifiable by their ways of life, their activities or their status: (1) totally destitute children, (2) vagrant children, (3) children of families living on pavements or in slums, (4) rag-pickers, (5) shoeshine boys, (6) illegal hawkers and porters working in stations and markets, (7) helpers in stations, (8) itinerant traders, (9) errand boys, (10) car-park boys, (11) procurers and (12) children of lepers and prostitutes.

These children naturally tend to prefer activities that give them the greatest chances of finding food: 22 per cent of them are coolies (dogsbodies), 10 per cent do petty jobs in hotels and 10 per cent pedal cycle-taxis.

To facilitate their work, DBAI professional workers classify children in difficult situations or street/working children in three categories depending on the nature of the relations that these children maintain with their families, their relationship with society in general and the rehabilitative approach to be chosen. A distinction is thus made between (a) street children, (b) vagrant children, and (c) delinquent children.

Street children

Under this general heading, DBAI makes a distinction between:
- Children 'in' the street or children who do petty jobs and who live in the street while maintaining regular contact with their families. For children in this category, who are usually the majority, return to the family remains the central aim of street life.

- Street children proper, fewer in number, who live and work in the street, which is their normal home. There they seek shelter, food and substitutes for the family atmosphere that they re-create with their peers. Few among them can maintain significant links with their families. Having much more difficulty in finding a job, they often indulge in delinquent practices and consequently have difficult relations with the police and society in general.

- Abandoned children (children without a family or neglected children) who, in their everyday activities, blend into the two previous categories. However, being deprived of all family links, they are left totally to themselves, materially and psychologically. They are particularly vulnerable and deserve special approaches in the work of rehabilitation.

Vagrant children

Generally aged 7 to 10, they are separated from their families for various reasons, have great interurban mobility, thanks to the railway, and manifest disorders in their interpersonal and social relations.

In this category a distinction is made between (a) vagrants of village origin, often with no home in Madras, and among whom are those who maintain contact with the village if they can, and (b) vagrants from established urban backgrounds who have left home for the street.

This latter group includes: (a) new vagrants who live by day in the street and sleep at home at night; (b) regular vagrants who still retain some contact with their parents; and (c) permanent vagrants or 'street-hardened' vagrants who, separated from their families, live a life constantly exposed to various risks.

Vagrant children from Madras have usually completely broken with their families, are highly mobile within the city, struggle for the basics of survival, possess few personal effects or none at all, engage in an everyday search for food, have a strong spirit of independence, are prone to aggressiveness, gambling and drug abuse, and suffer in encounters with older vagrants.

Delinquent children

These are children who have been arrested at least once by the police. They are a minority but constitute the most street-hardened category and the ones most resistant to dialogue with social workers.

Forced to provide for their own needs and those of their families, street children, of whatever category, devote long days – usually from 5 a.m. to midnight – to petty jobs in the informal sector (tea servers in small snack-bars, etc.) or real jobs in the formal sector – jobs rejected by adults because they are too hard or dangerous or because they are poorly paid (chef's assistant in restaurants, handling goods in the back of shops, etc.). The street child, daily occupied in such routine jobs, can rarely have any time to himself to devote to the normal needs of a child of his age, such as education, sport, etc.

The expression 'street children' is a word with many meanings. But one thing is certain: whatever the category, group or subgroup these young people belong to and so long as they are left to their own devices, they have a constant trap and vicious spiral before them. That spiral is marked by a series of interdependent causes with ever-growing complications, the most manifest of which are poverty, family breakdown, abandonment or becoming an orphan, the impossibility of satisfying needs vital to the physical, mental and emotional development of a child. Then there is a lack of education, schooling and vocational training, the necessity of accepting poorly paid, dangerous or dirty work, sacrifice of the pleasures of childhood, despair, delinquency, adult illiteracy later, emotional loneliness and unwanted procreation – resulting in the birth of children condemned, in advance, to live on the streets and hence in poverty, which is where it all started!

Don Bosco Anbu Illam

The DBAI institution was set up in 1978 by Joe Fernandez, a Hindu priest of the Catholic Salesian Don Bosco congregation. He had become aware of the situation of poor children in Madras, and first spent six years (1978–84) in a community development effort in the poor areas of the city before embarking on scientific research into the case of rag-pickers (or sorters and sellers of industrially recyclable articles: paper, plastic, glass, metals, etc.). But it was with his successor, Father Vincent Xavier, director of the institution since 1984, that Shelter Homes developed. There are now sixteen all over the city centre. In 1985 the first true well-furnished and well-appointed rehabilitation centre was opened for street children and working children, but more particularly for rag-pickers. In the same year, a second shelter home was opened, reserved primarily for illegal child porters at the central railway station. To get these children out of clandestine jobs, DBAI set up a rag-pickers co-operative for them in 1988 which was legalized in 1991. Meanwhile, in 1990, a third centre, the Don Bosco Anbu Illam Model Training/Rehabilitation Centre, was set up in co-operation with the Government of Tamil Nadu, in Royapuram district. This centre is strongly oriented towards vocational training and is solely reserved for street children and working children.

Structure of the institution

The central management of DBAI includes a chairman, a director, secretariat and an assistant director with an administrative department and an education department under his control. Each of these, in turn, is managed by an assistant. The education department includes: technical education; literacy training; arts and music; scouting; and ethics and other disciplines. Teaching is provided by central instructors from the shelter homes and by local teachers outside the homes. These teachers are aided by 'facilitators'. The administrative department includes an administrative unit and a unit attached to the co-operative for the sale of recyclable articles. These units are managed by a co-ordinator.

Aims and content of rehabilitation work

The principal aim of DBAI is the all-round development of the child. The work to achieve it consists essentially of activities aimed at protecting the child – in a situation involving risks, conflicts, disasters, abandonment or neglect – against the risks of exploitation in all its forms. The work consists also in combating the poverty surrounding the child and providing him with all the services that his situation requires. Depending on the case, action is conducted within the family or the community, working with the municipal authorities, the state of Tamil Nadu or the central government, the police and non-governmental organizations. The work consists finally of regularly alerting the public through the mass media, examining the situation of each child, organizing brain-storming sessions on important problems and producing documents for activities.

Work method

Currently, the social rehabilitation activities offered by DBAI cover 500 to 600 street and working children. Concretely, these activities take the form of: (a) contacts with children in the street or where they normally live; (b) taking them into a DBAI home where the work of rehabilitation continues; (c) rehabilitation work carried on directly in the street; (d) scientific research and general discussion about key issues; (e) preventive rehabilitation measures carried out in poor areas, streets and places where people live; (f) interacting with the public concerned – families, employers, the police, neighbours, parishioners, etc.; and (g) co-ordinating all these activities.

The work is carried out in three stages according to the particular features of each child or group of children. In the first, preparatory stage, an effort is made to get a clear view of the situation of each child and his or her problems and understand all interactions between child and society. This is achieved by:

- Making contact with the child, day or night, in the street, the shelter homes or centres for the sale of recyclable articles.
- Establishing links between the child and society and, to that end, appealing to the general goodwill, responding to the child's need for healthy and sustained human relations, and responding to any need for shelter, safety and the advantages of a stable job such as those offered by the sale of recyclable articles at the co-operative.

- Carrying out systematic and sustained supervision of each child throughout this stage. This supervision makes it possible to know the child's physical and mental needs, assess progress and settle on the most suitable work method for his or her case. The children themselves, along with their immediate circle, family, friends and employers, participate in this supervision.

The second stage, that of education and vocational training, includes programmes drawn up, almost individually, for: (a) learning reading, writing and arithmetic (or functional literacy); (b) vocational training; (c) job placement; (d) entry into a production and learning centre; and (e) enrolment in a formal educational establishment.

In the third or socio-economic integration stage, the work of rehabilitation, education and vocational training is completed by helping former street children, if they so wish, to take out a loan to build a house, get married and have a normal social life. In short, DBAI provides street children with the most useful services ranging from getting away from the street or exploitation to economic and social integration, and including, *inter alia,* education and information on the possibilities of a change of life.

From idea to action – services to children

Contact in the street

The social worker or street instructor uses any pretext that works to engage and maintain a dialogue with the child on every subject, on what interests him most. The immediate aim is to be able to make the child receptive to practical advice and to examine his or her situation and the range of possible services that DBAI offers in its shelter homes. This is to create and awaken in the child the desire to visit one of the homes.

Services in the shelter homes

On the very first visit to one of the sixteen homes, the street or working child will be able to take a good shower, have a good, cheap (subsidized) meal and take part in leisure activities in a clean environment.

Return to the family

If after conversations and examination of the situation and contact with a shelter home, the child asks to return to his family, DBAI identifies and studies all the problems, helps to resolve them (rectification or regularization of a marriage for example), gives the child advice and information, and lends money to help the child find a job.

If reintegration of the child into the family so requires, DBAI will help other members of the family in the same way.

Health care

So long as the child attends a shelter home, he or she will be able to benefit from medical checks and treatment from a group of doctors who specialize in different areas of medicine. Drug-abuse cases are looked after by specialist clinics. Health checks include monitoring the child's growth, diagnosing illnesses, special treatment for handicapped children, and requiring the child to keep body and surroundings clean.

At least 100 million children are threatened by drug addiction.

Photo: © UNICEF/Francene Keery

Safety

DBAI obtains an identity card issued by the Madras Police Commissioner for each of its children; this card, in theory, places them beyond the reach of police harassment while at the same time starting them out on the road to fulfilment. In the event of conflict with the law, DBAI attends the trial and helps the child in the legal process.

Leisure activities

It is not enough to attract children to rehabilitation centres; they also have to be kept there by activities that interest them. The shelter homes offer the children indoor and outdoor games, daily television broadcasts, weekly video-film shows, picnics, outings to the country, and cultural festivals and meetings.

Motivation camps

In addition to leisure and recreational activities, motivation camps lasting several days are specially organized, once a term, for homogeneous groups of children based on certain criteria: age or particular problems and needs identified through the systematic supervision mentioned above, etc. These camps offer the children the chance to learn to share a peaceful moment with other children, following different rules from those of the street. They make a pleasurable break from the regimented, monotonous and dangerous everyday existence and, by group activities within the framework of personality-training programmes, motivate the children.

Co-operative movement

This involves helping children who are rag-pickers (mainly paper) to organize themselves to sell their products directly to waste-recycling firms and escape the middlemen who exploit them. During the motivation camps, they get practical information about the laws of the market and how to make more profit through the co-operative.

Education

Basic education – that is all forms of education aimed both at primary-school-age children and illiterate adults – is one of the most important activities DBAI offers children through evening classes in the shelter homes and pavement schools, and in some cases with formal education in schools equipped with boarding facilities, civic and religious education. Juvenile delinquency, alcoholism and drug abuse are treated with understanding and firmness.

Technical and vocational training

This type of education includes carpentry, engineering, training to drive a variety of vehicles, tailoring, and on-the-job training and specialized training in various other trades.

Boys' town

This particular form of fostering combines a family atmosphere with the education of street children in need of foster families and unable to succeed in their studies at formal schools. Education and vocational training at DBAI's specialized centres which are educational structures adapted to the various personality traits peculiar to street children are discussed below.

Integration into economic and social life

With survival assured, and education and training accomplished, the process of rehabilitation begins to focus on its final objective of self-employment or paid employment. To that end, DBAI puts the 'former' street child in touch with employers if paid work is his priority problem. This makes marriage and the founding of a normal family possible.

Homes and specializations

Three of the sixteen Homes of Love have their own special feature in addition to survival and formal education. The Don Bosco Anbu Illam Model Training/Rehabilitation Centre (MTRC) stresses personality training and vocational training; the Don Bosco Anbu Illam Rag Pickers Society enables some children to provide for their needs financially under the supervision of DBAI, and the Don Bosco Anbu Illam Boys' Town looks after children with no family.

Don Bosco Anbu Illam – The Home of Love. Each home is placed under the responsibility of an assistant who co-ordinates activities. He reports daily on his activities to the DBAI assistant director and, occasionally to the director if need be. The assistant is helped by a night servant and a day servant. The homes are open round the clock so as to enable free access to children who work at night, such as those at the central railway station, or those who collect recyclable waste in the street by day. Street children who have not yet been recruited can frequent the homes freely and discover all the benefits they can derive from them. Recruitment for the homes is carried out – usually at night – by servants and by children already familiar with the home. Each recruited youngster has a file which is regularly updated and makes it possible to give him or her exactly the service that is needed. Functional literacy courses, for example, depend on the context of each child. Generally, the teaching of reading, writing and arithmetic takes place in the homes between 10 a.m. and noon and between 5.30 and 8 p.m.

DBAI Model Training/Rehabilitation Centre (MTRC). In addition to the all-round development of the street child and the working child, MTRC is especially designed to meet the aims of the second and third stages at DBAI, that is vocational training followed by integration into working life or further study or training. The infrastructure and equipment of the centre are designed to this end: large spaces, highly functional buildings and locations (recreation yard, playing field, shower rooms, staff area and meeting room, a fifty-bed dormitory, a refectory, a large classroom and workshops). Apart from the administrative staff, there are ten people who look after the children, including the assistant, the literacy teachers, a music teacher, a motor mechanic and driving instructor (tricycles, cars, etc.), a sewing instructor, a cook, a bursar and his assistant.

Basic education is offered to three categories of children: (a) illiterate children; (b) those who are already literate; and (c) those who have completed their technical training in the centre. To catch up with those in the second group, those in the first group are given intensive literacy courses. Those who pass the primary-school leaving examination organized by the Government of Tamil Nadu can either continue further studies in formal institutions or continue their technical training in the centre. At the end of the training course in the centre the children can again choose to enter the formal system or go further with their technical training and specialize in a given area. In the latter case, the centre places them in Don Bosco technical institutes equipped with boarding facilities or other institutes, as they desire. Children who have completed their training in the centre and do not wish to continue their studies in the formal academic system or in technical or vocational institutes are helped to find an income-generating occupation and accommodation. Their dependence on the centre is reduced to a minimum; nevertheless, they are free to continue coming there as part of an ongoing education that can lead to the acquisition of spoken and written English, the normal working language of the centre being Tamil.

Non-formal technical training consists in theoretical courses in the mornings and practical ones in the afternoons, sewing and how to maintain and repair vehicles, under effective supervision. After just a few days of being taught the rudiments of the trade, pupils work on orders for clothes and requests for maintenance or repair work from outside customers. To supplement their technical training, children are given classes in music (guitar, harmonium and tabla drum) and gardening.

Life in the centre is based on a number of principles and rules that can be summed up as respect and tolerance. Any street or working child admitted there has accepted a semi-structured life in an environment where a family atmosphere and informal behaviour prevail, an environment without strict discipline, where freedom and development are the cornerstones. But the counterpart of a semi-structured environment is a basic

framework of rules. For example, children get up at 6 a.m.; at
6.30 a.m., the task of maintaining the centre and other routine
jobs begin; at 7.30 a.m., prayer meeting; 8 a.m., breakfast,
classes, workshops; 12.30 p.m., lunch break; 2.30 p.m., classes,
practical work; 4 p.m., games; 6 p.m., individual study,
supplementary classes and activities (music, etc.); 8 p.m.,
evening meal, break; 9 p.m., 'goodnight' meeting during which
items of information are communicated and the programmes for
the following day are set out. There are discussions, singing and
prayers before going to bed. The most important principles
governing the staff are: (a) limitless patience in teaching and in
the process of transmitting knowledge and correcting habits;
(b) the instructor must constantly bear in mind the fact that,
because of the street child's age and previous experience, he will
need much more time to learn or change character than would a
'normal' child; (c) the instructor must be available, attentive and
easily accessible so as to be able to monitor and assess the
progress of each child; (d) the child must be given no corporal
punishment and must not be humiliated – if he deserves
criticism, this must never be given to him in public; (e) the child
must be encouraged to visit his family – if one exists and it does
not pose any particular problem – in the evenings, on Sundays or
during holidays; and (f) all the major religious and national
festivals must be celebrated as grandly as possible for these
deprived children who want the joys of 'normal' children too.

Vagrancy Prevention Programme (VPP)

This programme is based on the idea that the fight against the
phenomenon of street and working children must necessarily be

two-pronged: rehabilitation for children already victims of the phenomenon and prevention for children in danger of becoming so. The first fight will have no end if the second is not carried on in parallel. VPP attempts to identify how the problem might develop so that precautionary measures can be taken. To this end, the programme gives basic education and literacy classes in the evenings to children from the Madras slums and closely follows their educational progress. Slums are, obviously, the real breeding-grounds of street and working children. Every three months, VPP offers these children motivation camps and educational outings. The programme also pays the school fees for those children entering formal education and provides them with school uniforms, for it is often parents' inability to pay for these that prevents children from going to school. In 1992, this programme, with ten instructors, reached 300 children in five slums.

Don Bosco Anbu Illam Boys' Town

The aim of this educational structure is to give children with no family the parental attention and affection that they need by using the services of foster parents recruited and installed in small houses. They make up a campus comprising teaching areas called 'colleges'. Each college can take in a homogeneous group of fifteen to twenty children aged 10 to 18 who have already spent six months to a year in one of the Don Bosco Shelter Homes. In addition, to be recruited into the Boys' Town, the child must be potentially delinquent, potentially a street or working child. Usually these are children living in slums. The child must have the correct attitudes for living in a community;

he must be able to tolerate a structured educational or vocational training system for three years. Finally, any boy considered to be in a difficult situation by the Management of the Boys' Town can be admitted if he so desires. The classes given in the campus are government-recognized. They include formal educational programmes covering the whole primary cycle and the Production/Learning Centre (PLC). Here, the training is based on the same principles as those of the Model Training/Rehabilitation Centre described above. All the items produced are sold.

The Town is financed by the Don Bosco Salesian congregation, the Government of Tamil Nadu, the Ministry of Social Affairs, foreign agencies, business firms and individuals.

The reasons for such an initiative are well known. Formal schools with their organization, laws and rules cannot satisfy the psychological needs of street and working children, especially when they have no family. The lack of attention, passion for freedom, economic constraints and vagrant attitudes that typify these children prevent them from adapting to the formal system of education. Abject poverty, tense relations at home, the criminal subculture and the harmful phenomena of caste and religious beliefs deprive them of the pleasures of childhood. Experience has shown that putting these children in institutions is not a good solution either for them or for children in a difficult situation in general. In the cultural context in which they live, adoption is not possible either. The only solution to be recommended is this fostering formula.

The organization and administration of the Boys' Town are based on those of DBAI itself (director, assistant director, town co-ordinator, foster parents and child beneficiaries). The foster parents are directly responsible for the well-being of the children accommodated in the various cottages on the campus. They prepare meals for them, plan their education with them, follow the progress of each of them and duly report to the director. They meet the children's material and affective needs, thus playing for them the twin role of parents and teachers. To be recruited, the foster parents must be emotionally mature and happily married, have the ability to look after street children, be available, and have a sense of devotion and altruism.

Results

- Three well-equipped homes, situated in the heart of the city where children in difficult situations tend to congregate, offer their services to some 400 children.
- A model training/rehabilitation centre offers rehabilitation courses to some sixty children.
- Evening schools set up in five slums are attended by 300 children.
- 200 children supported by DBAI attend formal schools.
- Some 300 runaway children have been returned to their families.
- Twenty-five former participants in the courses have married and found permanent homes.
- Five homes have been built to accommodate former participants in the courses.
- Five shops of the paper co-operative have been linked together into a network to provide 200 members with better conditions for ensuring their future.
- 100 bank loans have been granted by the Indian Overseas Bank to promote self-employment and private trade.

- Thirty-five boys have learned to drive vehicles and thus have the chance of employment.
- Identity cards have been issued to all the children participating in the courses.

Nevertheless, numerous constraints persist. Firstly, rehabilitation is not always either rapid or successful. It is sometimes extremely difficult since a child's running away or vagrancy is not only a physical phenomenon but a psychological one too. The result is an existence characterized by brutality and agitation. Rehabilitation is a long-term process to be pursued until a true awakening begins. The uncontrolled desire by the instructors to obtain immediate results from the children and their firm commitment to the courses may, in the long run, turn against the children's interests.

Secondly, the inadequacy of material means it is hard to give an accurate picture of children in difficult situations. Eight other persisting constraints are: (a) the existence of standard contents in non-formal education courses; (b) harassment caused by vested interests and anti-social elements; (c) the absence of infrastructure such as buildings (classrooms, halls, etc.), playgrounds, hospitals, means of transport, etc.; (d) lack of staff-training courses; (e) inadequate financial support; (f) lack of serious, probing scientific research in this area; (g) absence of any spirit of co-operation among street-children employers; and (h) lack of responsibility on the part of parents.

Despite all these constraints, Don Bosco Anbu Illam remains one of the most comprehensive and innovative institutions acting in favour of children in difficulty. Not only does it addresses the whole of these children's essential needs, it also does so in terms of both survival and education. It apparently does not face any serious risk of disappearing or even declining in the near future, so unshakeable are the spiritual and moral foundations that underpin the commitment of those running it. It is certainly these solid foundations and ideas that enable them to rise above the ever-present financial worries.

Survival on the street

Save the Children Fund (UK) street children project,
Sri Lanka

Who and what are 'street children'? There must be as many
definitions as there are countries. For Save the Children Fund
(UK), whose street children project was launched in 1986, a
street child is any minor who is without a permanent home or
adequate protection. They live in extreme poverty. They are
homeless. Survival on the street, both day and night, is the only
option open to them. In Sri Lanka, most street families are to be
found in Colombo, but major towns such as Kandy and Galle
are also faced with similar problems.

The size of the problem

In its *Profile of Child Development in Sri Lanka,* the Department
of National Planning estimated that about 23 per cent of the
total population is composed of children under the age of 15. Of
these, some 10,000 are believed to live on the streets.

Almost half this number have never been to school and the
others are mostly primary-school drop-outs. Despite the fact
that education has been free in Sri Lanka for more than four
decades, only a small minority have had any experience of
secondary education.

Objectives

In broad terms, the aim of the project is to lay the foundations for lasting improvement in the socio-economic conditions of street children as well as seeing to their overall fulfilment.

In more specific terms this involves: (a) meeting immediate welfare needs, including food, shelter and security; (b) providing access to health and educational facilities, employment and housing, and discovering ways of helping street children to lead a productive life in their own environment; (c) helping to reinforce their ties with family and community life; and (d) developing their ability to take initiatives and build their own future.

The keys to success

The two key components of the project are the play groups and the day shelters. There are also literacy classes for the 6-to-14-year-olds, followed by vocational training classes for the 14-to-18-year-olds.

The day shelters act as 'drop-in centres' for street families. They are designed to show street families how to earn a basic or a supplementary income. They differ from the play groups in that they are accessible to children and young mothers at any time of the day. The importance of the play groups cannot be over-emphasized, since it is through them that participants are initially attracted to the project.

Street educators and project workers used to go looking for street families and encourage the parents to send their children to a play group in their area. Street families are now aware of the project and pass on the message to others.

Children who participate in project activities live in the heavily populated urban areas of Colombo and Kandy. Over half the children are Sinhalese, about a quarter are Tamil and the remainder are Muslim. Interaction between the children appears to be totally unaffected by these ethnic differences. In most cases, the language of communication, used both by the children and project workers, is Sinhalese.

Learning is child's play

The play-group scheme is based on 'learning through play'. At present there are six play groups in operation in Colombo, one in Kandy and one in Boralasgamuwa, each with between fifteen and twenty children under 5. They are usually open in the morning from 8.30 to 11.30 a.m.

The basic concept of the play group is that attendance is voluntary; there is absolutely no pressure to attend on any occasion. The focus is on 'learning through creative play'. Although commercially produced play materials are used, teachers are encouraged to produce simple, low-cost play material by recycling.

Play-group sessions are comprehensive yet unstructured. In addition to the play activities, the children all receive food supplements – consisting of a glass of milk and a mid-morning snack. Minor medical attention is at hand if needed. Those with more serious ailments are referred to medical centres for treatment. The children are also provided with clothing and are encouraged to develop regular habits of personal hygiene.

Equally important, the play group serves as a point of

contact with the children's parents, providing opportunities to advise them on such matters as nutrition, health care, social integration and managing the family budget. They can also be given advice on sexually transmitted disease, especially HIV/AIDS.

Literacy – the 'Open Sesame'

Literacy is a magic password that opens many doors; to employment, to a reasonable standard of living and, for the street children of Sri Lanka, to entry into the formal education system. Since virtually all the street children are illiterate, it was inevitable that literacy classes should figure among the project's activities. Contact was made with the non-formal-education branch of the Ministry of Education and, with its approval, three-hour literacy classes are provided, three times a week, at four centres, for children 6 to 14. These literacy classes for children not in school are to help young people gain admission to the formal school system at the grade appropriate to their age.

Save the Children Fund (UK) also provides clothing, school-books and other necessities for children from play groups moving into formal school as well as for the sufficiently literate and older children who can attend formal school while still living on the streets.

At first there was some reluctance to admit street children into the formal school system, but, once admitted, they performed well. School officials now have no hesitation in allowing street children to enter their schools.

Administrative headaches

Despite the goodwill of the school officials, administrative difficulties remain. The main problem has been that many street children do not know their date of birth, and birth certificates are often unavailable or have been lost. This causes a lot of difficulty since a birth certificate is a prerequisite for entry into any school in Sri Lanka.

Faced with this problem, project workers arrange for a literate street child, wanting to enter formal school, to be examined by a qualified doctor. The latter can then make an estimate of the child's age and a Certificate of Probable Age is issued by the Registrar General.

The project worker has to trace the missing birth certificate as rapidly as possible for the child needs official confirmation of his or her age in order to take part in certain sporting activities and, later, when seeking employment.

The educators

It takes dedication, ceaseless effort and abundant patience to train and educate street children. About half a dozen staff (leader, project officer, teachers, vocational-training instructors and helpers) are employed at each day shelter. These dedicated men and women (mostly women) constitute the heart and soul of the project.

Staff range in age from about 24 to 45 and most play-group teachers have been through a pre-school teacher-training programme. Save the Children Fund (UK) also runs a compulsory, permanent, in-house educational training course to keep workers informed of the latest trends in management and communication and the concept of 'learning through play'.

One continuing cause for concern is the low remuneration of staff. There is no official salary structure or consistent wage scale and the salary paid to one leader may differ from that paid to another depending on the centre.

While the overall management and monitoring of the project is the responsibility of Save the Children Fund (UK), the thirty-five workers who deal directly with the street children come from associated non-governmental organizations. It is important that the skills of child-care workers, for educating street children or not, be adequately recognized and paid accordingly.

Learning a trade

Street children do not need any previous educational base to follow the vocational training courses available at the project centres. They merely have to attend classes where the curriculum focuses on functional literacy.

The training itself emphasizes the practical rather than the theoretical aspects of the course. Older children and young adults can take part in skills-development programmes in woodwork, welding, dressmaking and tailoring under the supervision of qualified instructors.

In all the project's educational and vocational training programmes an attempt is made to take individual talents, motivation and specific interests into consideration. The instructors can arrange for pupils to receive additional tutoring or to follow a more advanced course.

Individual support is given to insecure children who may

have problems adapting to the projects' educational and vocational training environment. Staff have been trained to give limited support to children with emotional problems and to recognize when a child needs to be referred to a specialist.

The vocational training activities of the project are very similar to those in any other formal institution. They differ in that the training is wholly voluntary and balanced between theoretical and practical content. The project favours a more comprehensive, practically oriented curriculum with minimum theory as the street children have expressed difficulty in accepting intensive theoretical training.

State recognition

From the beginning of January 1993, the Sri Lankan National Apprenticeship Board decided to issue a certificate of competency to anyone completing the prescribed courses at the Skills Development Unit of the Borella day shelter. Older children who follow these courses will receive a monthly allowance to cover travel expenses to the Borella day shelter.

National recognition of the project's vocational training is a considerable achievement. It is particularly encouraging not only because it confirms the quality of the project training scheme but also because it demonstrates the government's favourable attitude towards the entire project. When a pupil completes a training course and is ready to start work, a basic tool kit is provided from project funds.

However, that successful completion of a vocational training course brings no guarantee of employment. A number of young people who have completed one of these courses are still looking

Many successful projects teach street children outside the premises of the traditional school.

Photo: *Dominic Sansoni*

for jobs and the project has as yet not identified ways of helping them find employment. This is a matter to which particular attention is now being devoted. One of the biggest problems is that potential employers are often deterred because of social misconceptions about street children and ex-street children being undisciplined, thieving vagrants.

The day shelters

The day shelters for street children and their families have become thriving, independent communities in which everyone is encouraged to participate. Two day shelters are currently in operation – one in Colombo, the other in Kandy. For three years, from 1987 to 1990, they were run as night shelters to provide temporary accommodation for street mothers desperate for somewhere to live. It soon became apparent, however, that the two shelters could not possibly cope with the increasing flood of applicants. Street mothers were staying on as lodgers for very long periods. The system was clearly not in the long-term interest of street families. Instead of using the shelters as a springboard for family advancement, they were becoming dependent upon them.

The hard decision was taken to abandon the residential approach and to use the buildings as multiple-role day shelters functioning as: a crisis intervention centre to help families in dire need of immediate assistance; a child-care facility so mothers could leave their pre-school age children while working or looking for work; a vocational training facility for both parents and children; and an initial point of contact or haven from the street environment.

Both shelters operate a child-care facility with pre-school

activities (for children 3 to 5), afternoon literacy classes for older children (6 to 14), skills-development sessions for adolescents (14 to 18) and a community library. The mothers of street children are also free to attend the literacy classes.

One of the aims of the day shelters is to enable street children and their families to attain the status of semi-skilled workers. The staff at the shelters have succeeded in securing employment for some twenty mothers, including posts as hospital attendants, garment-factory workers and traffic attendants. Others work in income-generating activities such as soft-toy making, patchwork sheets, children's clothes and incense sticks to sell on the streets.

The street children and their families are encouraged to participate in all aspects of the day shelters, both at a practical level and also in terms of self-determined organization and planning. The shelters have a multi-faith approach, with all religions encouraged to integrate freely. Save the Children Fund (UK) encourages various governmental and non-governmental organizations and agencies to participate in the day-to-day management of activities at each centre.

Housing

By definition, housing is one of the most difficult problems facing street families. Urban accommodation is almost universally in short supply, but the street families also have to overcome the social prejudices which label them as unsuitable and unreliable tenants.

In 1991, the National Housing Development Authority of Sri Lanka launched a special scheme under which street families were given small plots of land and financial grants (10,000 rupees per family) towards the cost of building houses. This was supplemented by a matching grant from Save the Children Fund (UK). Eight project families benefited from this scheme which, unfortunately, is no longer operating.

The maximum housing aid the project is now able to provide is 2,000 rupees. This would assist a street family to pay the rent and purchase the basic amenities needed to set up a home. To date, some seventy families have been assisted in this way.

A loan scheme helps former street families to continue to pay rent and to make a living for themselves. The loans are repayable in small, interest-free instalments. The scheme is also available to other street families to enable them to set up small business enterprises and eventually to become self-supporting.

Street families given financial assistance are obliged to place at least 20 rupees a month, per child, in a saving scheme operated through the National Savings Bank of Sri Lanka. Since 1991, project workers have arranged savings accounts for around 200 street families.

Funding

The manner in which the street children project is funded reflects the general enabling strategy. This strategy emphasizes responsibility based on the participation of beneficiaries who, rather than being regarded as recipients of charity, are seen as partners in a form of assisted self-help.

The basic aim is to help street children lead healthy, productive lives in their own environment rather than to remove them from it and place them in a situation of total dependency. To this end, Save the Children Fund (UK) works closely with partner agencies. Although at present it bears 90 per cent of the total responsibility for running the activities at the Colombo and Kandy day shelters, a 'fade-out' strategy has been adopted under which there will be a phased hand-over of management and financial responsibility to partner agencies. Partner agencies have, for example, already taken over the responsibility for paying grants to the shelters, although they have to follow agreed guidelines and expenditure has to be accounted for.

The cost of educational play material, kitchen equipment and other supplies, as well as any emergency expenditure, is met by Save the Children Fund (UK). These costs include the funding of parties held for the children, at the various centres, for the New Year celebrations. Practical gift packs are given to each child.

Follow-up

If its projects are to be both sustainable and worth while, Save the Children Fund (UK) is very much aware of the need to learn from experience. Research studies on street children are carried out periodically, and experiences and results are carefully documented. The decision taken to change from night shelters to day shelters is an example of a strategy mutation resulting from practical experience as investigation showed that night shelters led to increasing dependency. Children were originally found by project workers when meeting and talking to street families. Now that the project is well established, however, information about the programmes offered is passed on among street families by word of mouth. Attendance is regular and the drop-out rate is very low.

Set up and fade out

The scale of the problem of street children, not only in Sri Lanka but throughout the world, is such that there is a great temptation to see it as a problem that can only be tackled by massive governmental intervention on a national scale.

Unfortunately, most governments have neither the resources nor the expertise to assume this responsibility. Furthermore, social engineering by government decree is slow, politically difficult to implement and is often seen, even by those who stand to gain most from it, as being an unwarranted interference in the lives of citizens.

The problem can really only be satisfactorily handled by self-governed initiatives that offer a complete package of assistance. Above all the programmes must remain small enough to retain their personal touch and avoid being seen as charity.

Most disadvantaged groups resent charity and accept it only grudgingly. What they want is the feeling that somebody cares and is prepared to help them help themselves. It would be an error, therefore, to judge the success of a project solely on the basis of the number of street children reinserted into society.

The success of the street children project is due to the fact that it meets these criteria: it offers a complete aid package on a partnership basis; it has clearly-defined objectives, which are subject to regular review; and it adopts a pragmatic approach to the achievement of these objectives. The self-perpetuating 'set up and fade out' strategy adopted by the Sri Lanka project shows great promise and might well be copied by other projects. As part of this strategy, Save the Children Fund (UK) is providing funds for the establishment of small businesses to help partner agencies generate their own income as the Fund aims eventually to withdraw its financial support.

For the children themselves, the project offers a unique overall package of commitment. Their most pressing needs, health care, food, clothing and, just as important, emotional security and self-confidence, are met through their voluntary participation in the play groups and day shelters. Educational and vocational training further enhances their development and their likelihood of finding employment.

Most significant of all, perhaps, is that the project has demonstrated the effectiveness of community-based care as opposed to long-term residential care. Children are discovering that it is possible to develop and succeed within the framework of their own families and communities.

Conclusions

As we suggested in the Introduction, the volume and the aim of this work – the professional exchange of information based on eighteen studies – has not allowed us to present any analysis, theory, or ready-made lesson to be applied in each case. It is up to the specialist or professional to draw his or her own conclusions. Even at the end of the work, however, certain observations need to be added.

The number of children helped by most of the projects – several hundred by project – is very small in view of the 100 million or more street and working children living around the world. It is also fair to say, that the number of children taken on by each educator in the projects, rarely more than ten, is also extremely limited in comparison with the numbers in formal education. For non-professionals in this area, the figures might seem disappointing and make any rehabilitation project seem absurd. This is not really the case though. Given the extent of the problem, one might feel more reassured if there were massive financial programmes with rapid results each year and thousands of children escaping their pitiable condition.

Yet experience shows us that such gigantic projects would not be effective. One can see why. These children, more than most, need a particularly intense and continuous form of attention and affection. The educator, therefore, needs to have a special and personal involvement, as well as an extremely solid competence, of the kind that is not necessarily found in universities but reached after long years of practical and pragmatic action. It is rare to find such a commitment coupled with professional capacity in one person, and this limits the number of possible qualified educators. The educator, in this domain, can only be efficient if he or she takes on a minimal number of children. So, whereas in the formal education system, a single teacher would be enough, two or three are needed to educate street children.

The children themselves, especially those who have previously dropped out of school, are not easy to lure into an informal educational programme, all the more so, when there is no official certificate at the end of it. Even the better known projects such as the Undugu Society (Kenya), the Atelier Bon Conseil (Togo) or the Don Bosco Anbu Illam (India) need special methods to recruit children and prevent too many from dropping out.

Some children only stay in the projects for a short while before rejoining their families, school or other formal professional training institutions. Moreover, the financing of projects relies essentially on private donations, which are always insufficient. This, too, limits the projects' capacity. Through these constraints and limits, one appreciates the sheer size of the educational work and the parallel investment needed if one wants to solve this problem, once and for all, or at least to slow down its increase.

On the positive side, thanks to the considerable number of non-governmental organizations working in this area, the total number of children throughout the world being helped is not as paltry as it seems. In the city of Rio de Janeiro alone there are an estimated 600 organizations, many of which have rehabilitation centres. This is the case in most large cities where the problem is serious enough.

The fact remains, nevertheless, that it is only by strong commitment from governments in identifying or combating the underlying causes, and in the implementation and financing of preventive and rehabilitation measures, that valid solutions will really be created.

The fight against the street-child phenomenon is a major aspect of any economic and social policy and, for that very reason, necessitates closer scrutiny. Conventional education systems should also apply preventive measures in the hope of giving greater flexibility to their structures and thereby stop children from dropping out. The originality of a number of projects for school children could serve as a model in the reorganization of formal education. Beyond the rehabilitation of poor peri-urban areas, the true prevention of the problem lies further, in the field of social policies, in the tackling of poverty in these zones. The promotion of such policies needs support from governments and national movements; it also needs children to be educated about their own rights.

It is hoped that the cases presented here will bear fruit in terms of creative imagination, professional efficiency and international solidarity. The mutual ideal of fraternity and justice that drives these groups and people, already engaged in the fight against this intolerable situation, is very hopeful.